I0039701

US-India Forward Leap–
The Partnership Building

US-India Forward Leap–
The Partnership Building

V. Rangaraj
Former Advisor – Corp. Strategy & Business Development
Aditya Birla Group
Founder Chairman – U.S. India Importers Council (USIIC)
Mumbai, India

Vaibhavi Palsule
Vice Principal – Ramnarain Ruia College
and Head of Dept. – Political Science
Ramnarain Ruia College, Mumbai, India

Allied Publishers Pvt. Ltd.
NEW DELHI • MUMBAI • KOLKATA • CHENNAI • NAGPUR
AHMEDABAD • BANGALORE • HYDERABAD • LUCKNOW

Allied Publishers Private Limited

Regd. Off.: 1/13-14 Asaf Ali Road, **New Delhi** – 110002
Ph.: 011-23239001 • E-mail: delhi.books@alliedpublishers.com

87/4, Chander Nagar, Alambagh, **Lucknow** – 226005
Ph.: 0522-4012850 • E-mail: appltdlko9@gmail.com

17 Chittaranjan Avenue, **Kolkata** – 700072
Ph.: 033-22129618 • E-mail: cal.books@alliedpublishers.com

15 J.N. Heredia Marg, Ballard Estate, **Mumbai** – 400001
Ph.: 022-42126969 • E-mail: mumbai.books@alliedpublishers.com

60 Shiv Sunder Apartments (Ground Floor), Central Bazar Road,
Bajaj Nagar, **Nagpur** – 440010
Ph.: 0712-2234210 • E-mail: ngp.books@alliedpublishers.com

F-1 Sun House (First Floor), C.G. Road, Navrangpura,
Ellisbridge P.O., **Ahmedabad** – 380006
Ph.: 079-26465916 • E-mail: ahmbd.books@alliedpublishers.com

751 Anna Salai, **Chennai** – 600002
Ph.: 044-28523938 • E-mail: chennai.books@alliedpublishers.com

Hebbar Sreevaishnava Sabha, Sudarshan Complex-2, No. 24/1, 2nd Floor,
Seshadri Road, **Bangaluru** – 560009.
Ph.: 080-22262081 • E-Mail: bngl.books@alliedpublishers.com

3-2-844/6 & 7 Kachiguda Station Road, **Hyderabad** – 500027
Ph.: 040-24619079 • E-mail: hyd.books@alliedpublishers.com

Website: www.alliedpublishers.com

© 2017, Authors

No part of the material protected by this Copyright notice may be reproduced
or utilized in any form or by any means, electronic or mechanical including
photocopying, recording or by any information storage and retrieval system,
without prior written permission from the copyright owners.

Published by Sunil Sachdev and printed by Ravi Sachdev at
Allied Publishers Pvt. Ltd., (Printing Division), A-104 Mayapuri Phase II,
New Delhi-110064.

Foreword

This book is a scholarly study of the evolution of the relationship between India and US, particularly in this millennium. As the authors say, the emerging positive relationship is due not only to the change in the perceptions of key policy-makers in the two countries, but also the emerging economic and technological strength of India.

The institutionalization of the Indo-US economic relations over the years is arguably one of the best parts of the book, and reflects the deep knowledge of the subject of one of the authors. A considerable part of the book is devoted to high technology. There is reference to the Indo-US nuclear agreement, the Indian software industry, and the fact that several Indian-Americans are now CEO's of some of the world's leading American technology companies. The book contains valuable statistics on a number of topics, which would be useful to scholars.

The contents of the Book are an interesting mix of economics, trade, foreign relations, the strategic dimension and technology, and of course reflect the perceptions of the authors on a complex subject. The book is up to-date, and analyses the implications of the Make in India policy of Prime Minister Modi and also comments on the recent inward-looking policy of the US under President Donald Trump.

I am sure that the book would appeal greatly to the general reader. The backgrounds of the two authors, Dr. Rangaraj with his variegated experience in commerce and industry and Dr. Palsule with her academic background in Political Science, have synergized effectively to bring out this remarkable and unique book.

Dr. R. Chidambaram
Principal Scientific Adviser to the Govt. of India
&
Chairman, Scientific Advisory Committe to the Cabinet
(Former Chairman, Atomic Energy Commission)

Preface

The US and India are friendly Nations and a symbol of World's largest free market democracies. During the past several years this bilateral relationship has been one of the most complex and difficult aspects of international politics. However, the US India relationship has withstood the test of times in its long journey. Changes in the business scenario driven by technology and developments in the geopolitical area compelled both the Nations to undertake a pragmatic assessment. Thus a new basis of relationship emerged in the form of economic and strategic engagements. Several books and monographs, research articles, newspaper analysis have been attempted in India and in the United States to explain the complex relationship.

This Book places its central theme and focus on Economic Engagement of India and US. The Author served the US Foreign Commercial Service for several years before embarking on a career in the Corporate Sector. The Co-author is a Professor of Political Science with long experience and has observed various developments in Indo-US Relations very closely over a period of time.

This Book is a most recent work on the Indo US Relations as the book opens up with the arrival of President Donald Trump to the White House. It further brings back developments that took place under President George Bush, President Obama, Prime Minister Manmohan Singh and current Prime Minister Shri Narendra Modi who gave a new strategic and security dimension to this relationship.

During the course of the economic engagement, challenges were faced at every stage and both the countries came out of tricky situations all the time. We have covered extensive information about the investment regime in both US and India and included case studies of six to seven leading Indian Companies and their investments in the US.

The present Book is a product largely of 8 months of intensive study, travel and interviews by both the author and the co-Author. It is a readymade Compendium for Indo US Policy and Decision Makers, including scholars and students and the business communities both in India and the US to gain perspective on the Economic Engagement in our relationship.

Dr. V. Rangaraj
Dr. Vaibhavi Palsule

Acknowledgement

This book was conceived during my several interactions and participation in the US India Business council Annual General Meetings held in Washington in June of 2015. I am indebted to the Aditya Birla Group (ABG), its Chairman Mr. Kumaramangalam Birla, Mrs. Rajashree Birla, Chairperson, CSR & Community Development, Mr. A.K. Agarwala, Chairman Business Review Council, ABG for the opportunity they gave me in associating with them and supporting me in this Venture.

I would like to thank the facilitative support provided to me by Mr. Moiez Lokhandwala, Managing Director, Lokhandwala Infrastructure Limited in completion of this book.

My Mentor and Guide Mr. Raymond E. Vickery (Former Assistant Secretary of Commerce, Clinton Administration) who helped me to give shape to this Book based on his vast experience in Indo US Relations.

Principal Dr. Suhas Pednekar (Ramnarain Ruia College, Mumbai, India) who was kind enough to introduce me to Prof. Dr. (Mrs.) Vaibhavi Palsule, Head, Department of Political Science, who helped me right from the initial stages of the Book, and ultimately became my co-author for this Book. Prof. Vaibhavi is a Research Scholar familiar with the subject. She contributed immensely for this Book.

Dr. Ramesh Babu, Former Head of the Department of Politics & Civics in Mumbai University, who was kind enough to review my material in the initial stages of the Book.

Mr. Rick Rossow, CSIS, Washington DC helped me to access data from variety of sources and in organizing interviews with Mr. Wadhwani and other entrepreneurs based in the US.

I would like to thank Mr. Dev Bhattacharya, Group EVP, Corporate Strategy & Business Development, ABG for providing me the encouragement and support.

In ample measure I would like to thank Mr. Harish Mehta, Founder President, NASSCOM who shared his valuable insights on the subject that gave us access to various charts and graphs from NASSCOM.

I would like to thank the staff of Indian Embassy, Washington who were extremely kind enough to provide direction for the Book.

I would like to thank Mrs. Aarti Desai, Chief Librarian, Nehru Centre Mumbai and Commodore Bhagat, and Mrs. Habbu from the Wellingdon Sports Club for making available their library facilities for reference work. I also like to thank Mr. Anil Datar of TISS, Mumbai who provided library paper support for this Book.

Mrs. Ajitha Panicker helped me to identify the Printers and Publishers for the book working closely with CA Subramanian.

At the US India Business Council, (USIBC), Ms. Diane Farell, now Dy. Asstt. Secretary of Commerce who understood the deep relationship between the economic interests of USIBC members helped us in the initial stages of the book.

Mr. Pranav Dongre and Mr. Sunil Dongre, Balchandra Printing Press who helped me with the manuscripts rearranging in different formats.

The first person to type the Book was my beloved Wife Saraswathi who was quite experienced as a copy editor having spent many years in corporate communications played a stellar role in publishing this Book.

My daughter Sukanya and her Husband Atman supported my thought for publishing the Book.

This book would have not been possible without the support of many others who have directly or indirectly contributed to the production of the Book.

Contents

Introduction

Review of Economic Engagement of India and US

Relationship between India and US has been passed through various phases since the emergence of India. After India's independence, US presumed India to be the prominent player in Asia and desired to develop closer relationship with India. However, India chose to distance itself from US due to the cold war that had just begin, and its ideological leaning towards socialism—socialist influenced planned economy and extensive state control of economy resulting in limited international economic engagement. Trade and investment between US and India was all time low and US-India economic engagement remain limited to aid. In the next two decades India got closer to erstwhile USSR and entered into a treaty of peace and friendship with USSR in 1971. India's heavy dependence on USSR, for arms and technological and financial aid for industry and infrastructure branded India as a Soviet Ally. The political and strategic compulsions of the cold war period brought US and Pakistan and later even US and China closer to each other. During this period, the economic instruments of engagement were used as instruments of pressure for political gains. For e.g. in the decade of 1960s, in return of wheat shipments to India, US brought pressure on India to start the peace talks with Pakistan, forced India to comply with agricultural reforms and curb any criticism of US engagement in Vietnam War. After the Indian nuclear tests of 1974, US adopted a policy of controlling technological exports (related to nuclear and missile technology). It was a coordinated effort with other nations. Thus the US-India relationship followed the pattern of "isolate or ignore" and it did not improve till the end of cold war.

Post-Cold War Period

End of cold war and the disintegration of Soviet Union brought significant changes in the world politics as a whole and in Indian politics specifically. Rising prices of oil due to first Gulf war, return of Indians working in Gulf, thus limiting the flow of foreign currency and the weak economy brought economic crises to the forefront. India had to open up its economy to overcome the massive economic crises and to keep pace with global economy. US was the economically dominant power, so India did not have any option but to develop closer relationship with US. Only US could satisfy India's need for huge FDI and urgency to repay a larger amount of loan. On the other hand US was also in search of a big potential market and India could satisfy this need of US. This brought India and US into a strategic partnership based on the shared interests of both—India's need for rapid economic growth and US need for a lucrative market and a candidate for foreign investment. Though, there was a positive environment for developing India-US relations in the immediate aftermath of cold war, one major impediment remained—India's firm stand over the non-proliferation issue. India with its own moral commitment towards nuclear disarmament, continued to hold a stand that it will not sign NPT on the ground of its discriminatory nature. The US pressure on India continued to mount which made India to prepare itself to become a Nuclear Weapons State. Finally India conducted nuclear tests in 1998, causing a negative phase in Indo-US relations—US economic sanctions against India. Pr. Clinton's visit to India in 2000 diluted this strain in the relationship between the two. And in the new millennium, India-US relations began to improve significantly.

The New Millennium

In the new millennium, India and US began to get engaged in different areas. The economic growth of India in the post reform period was the most important driving factor in increasing the official engagement between India and US. After reforms two way trade between India and US increased from $5.3 billion in 1990 to $12 billion in 1999.[1] There were approximately 300 Indian American entrepreneurs, many in high technology sector, and 774 Indian-American companies in Silicon Valley alone in 2000.[2] The active Indian-American politicians played an important role in relaxation of US sanction after Indian nuclear tests of 1998 and are also said to be the backbone of Indo-US nuclear deal in 2005. Also the role of Indian-Americans is advancing in American politics reaching them to the position of Governor is a major development. The Indian American community expanded by 69% between 2000 and 2010[3] and they are involved primarily in the information technology industry. The Indian Americans have been the high achievers in important fields.

[1] Dr. Stephen Cohen, "India and America–An emerging leadership" a paper presented at the conference, Dec 8-10, 2000, Kyoto, Japan.
[2] Ibid.
[3] Robert G. Sutter, "The United States and Asia: Regional dynamics and 21st century relations" page no. 235.

The positive relationship between India and US is not merely the result of changing geo-strategic equations in the post-cold war period, but also due to the change in the perceptions of key policy makers in both India and US. Though, the strains developed in India-US relations after Indian nuclear tests of 1998, the Vajpayee Government continued with its policy of maintaining good relations with West. Indo-US relations all these years revolved around only few issues prominently nuclear proliferation and US lack of sensitivity about the security concerns of India and many other areas where cooperation would be possible were neglected. However, during Kargil conflict, United States did not support its traditional ally—Pakistan, and almost forced Pakistan to withdraw Pakistani forces from LOC. This US stand demonstrated the change in the perception of US towards India and Pakistan. It was now clear that US was not ready to help Pakistan at the expense of India. Pr. Clinton's approach during Kargil conflict also signalled that, US perceives India as a partner in the new global order. After Pr. Clinton's visit in March 2000, the vision of a new relationship between India and US was developed that laid the foundation of bilateral relationship and partnership between India and US in the 21st century. In September 2000, Prime Minister Vajpayee declared in his speech in Asia society in New York that India and US were natural allies.[4] This signified that India was also interested in forward looking dialogue with US. Though US imposed sanctions, the representatives of US and India—Strobe Talbot and Jaswant Singh initiated a dialogue to reconcile India's security concerns with the non-proliferation objectives of US which led to the better

---

[4] Shukla, Subhash. Foreign policy of India. Anamika Pub & Distributors, 2007, page 250.

understanding of India's security concerns by US. Both also agreed for broad-based cooperation in the area of counter-terrorism.

Under Pr. Bush, India and US reiterated their commitment to complete the process of qualitatively transforming India-US relations. The Bush administration lifted the sanctions imposed by Clinton administration after 1998 nuclear tests. There was an agreement over expanding defence cooperation between two countries and cooperation on combatting international terrorism. In keeping with the intention of developing a strategic partnership with India, US and India entered into an agreement—"Next Step in Strategic Partnership" in January, 2004. Both the countries agreed to extend cooperation in the areas of civilian nuclear technology, space exploration, missile defence, and high technology trade. The further landmark development was Bush Administration's decision to pursue nuclear energy deal with India. India was technically ineligible for such deal as it had not signed NPT neither it had acceded to IAEA safeguards. In spite of this, it was Pr. Bush personal interest in India-US reapproachment which proved to be instrumental for this deal.

These agreements by America were based on its own assessment that, by 2025 India would be one of the world's five largest economies, having an enormous pool of highly educated and young people which would establish India as a force to reckon with in the 21st century.[5]

In the last ten years, India-US relationship has developed into a global strategic partnership, based on increasing

[5] Ibid page 261.

convergence of interests on bilateral, regional and global issues.[6] The bilateral relationship is getting strengthened due to cooperation in multiple sectors that include trade and investment, defence and security, science and technology, clean energy and environment, agriculture and health and education. As President Bush had put it "India and the United States are separated by half a globe. Yet, today our two nations are closer than ever before."[7]

Currently, the relations between India and US seem to have taken a new turn under President Trump. The closeness of India-US relations has come under question because of the different perspectives of the India and US leaders. India is trying to increasingly integrate with the international order and America under President Trump is showing the signs of withdrawal from international order. If US makes this strategy, its long term policy, there is every possibility that China will get more space to spread its dominance which can prove to be detrimental to Indian interests. However, there is a high possibility that this phenomena is short-lived. The relations between US and India are in such a stage that total about turn of this relationship will be unlikely. There may emerge some strains and ups and downs in the relationship, but in the long run the traditional liberal US values will help grow the relations between the two largest democracies of the world.

---

[6] http://www.mea.gov.in/Portal/ForeignRelation/India-U.S._Relations.pdf visited 11 June 2016.

[7] S. Paul Kapur and Sumit Ganguly, The Transformation of US-India Relations—An Explanation for the Rapprochement and Prospects for the Future (http://cisac.fsi.stanford.edu/sites/default/files/Kapur_Transformation_of_U.S._India_Relations.pdf) visited 11 June 2016.

Though, Indo-US relationship appears to be very promising at the moment, there are several grey areas. One is the US approach towards China. US sees India to be a potential balancer of China. It therefore expects that India's relationship with China should be in line with US policy towards China. However, India will frame its China policy according to its own foreign policy priorities and not in accordance with the US foreign policy goals. And the policies of India and US may not be compatible. Further India's troubled relations with South Asian neighbours especially Pakistan puts a lot of strain on Indian economy. The continued problem with neighbours force the diversion of resources required for development to the purpose of security. Also there are several complaints about the human rights violations against India. Human rights issue may prove to be a block in the progress of India-US relations.

Another important problem area is Indian economy. Though Indian economy shows impressive performance, deep-rooted inequality, poverty, and lack of basic resources in the rural areas are the persisting problems. The economic growth is primarily seen in the urban areas. The additional problem is the facilities and quality of public education system. Even the compatibility of standards of higher education is another area of concern. The lack of infrastructure and transportation facilities has negatively affected the growth of agricultural sector in India. Despite economic liberalization, Indian economy is still under several regulations which is a major problem in economic expansion. This weakness of Indian economy may impede economic growth. If these problems persist, India may not remain attractive strategic partner.

CHAPTER 1

Phenomenal Victory of President Trump

Mr. Donald Trump, a Republican Candidate got elected through a popular vote against Ms. Hillary Clinton (Democratic) on an unanticipated development and emerged as a Victor on November 27, 2016. Thus a new era dawned in the annals of American History where a billionaire businessman emerged as the 45th President of United States. Based on his election propaganda and his theme "Make America Great Again" the US Presidential elections, created ripples in World Capitals especially in India. The well-known TIME Magazine described the campaign of 2016 will be remembered for many things, but surely high among them was the constant experience of surprising alarm and alarming surprise.

A popular American Political Analyst described the Presidential race "efforts to undermine the democratic norms and institutions of our country—from the Republican nominee, who prided himself on breaking rules, to a Democratic nominee who often campaigned from a distant cocoon".[8]

---

[8] Nancy Gibbs, "Covering History" Nov 10, 2016 http://time.com/4565962/covering-history/accessed on 14/04/17.

THE RESULTS: CONGRESS

THE NEW SENATE

34 seats up for grabs
Democratic efforts to take control of the
Senate flopped. Early data showed the
party on course to pick up two seats, well
short of the five required to reclaim the
chamber majority.

46
Democrat

2
Independent *

51
Republican

1 unknown

DEMOCRATIC CONTROL

REPUBLICAN CONTROL

Seats won

12   21

*BOTH CAUCUC WITH DEMOCRATS

'I will be one hell of a check and balance on him.'

CATHERINE CORTEZ
MASTO, Democratic
Senator-elect for
Nevada, speaking
about President-
elect Donald Trump
after defeating
Representative Joe
Heck; Masto will be
the first ever Latina
Senator in Congress

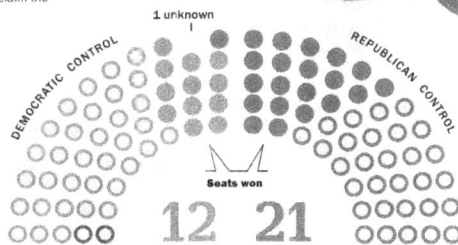

MISSOURI
In a difficult
contest, GOP
incumbent **Roy
Blunt** resisted a
challenge from
Army veteran
Jason Kander, a
top Democratic
recruit, 49%
to 46%

'This is a lot better than the last time I did one of these in Miami.'

MARCO RUBIO, Republican Senator from Florida,
joking about his most recent big address—a
speech announcing the end of his presenditial
run—after rebuffing a challenge from Democratic
Representative Patrick Murphy

Source: American Library, New Delhi

The divide that exists in the American Society, between wealthy and educated workers on one hand and manual working class vividly showed up in the Polls of Trump and Clinton Voters. Trump's Communication Advisor Mr. Jason Miller said in an interview that "there are two types of Americans after all, and one of them demanded to have its voice heard. The task of Trump campaign was to tap this seething populist distrust of the nation's elites, and they had no other foil than Clinton."[9] From the beginning Trump projected himself as a disruptive individual, his campaign staff compared him to "Uber". He had authenticity. He could draw big crowd. He could make statements. Often outrageous and regularly false-that would spread through the media and social networks like wildfire. Trump's first Campaign Manager Mr. Corey said he was what the wizards of Silicon Valley call a Platform: something new that people did not know they needed and which everyone could use as they wished.

In the words of Ms. Kellyanne Conway, Trump's Media Manager, "Trump mowed down every challenge. It was his message, his vision, his stubbornness and bombast that changed the country". Trump was the one who picked up immigration and trade as his signature issues. He recognized the populist tide waiting to be unleashed. If he stopped tweeting and started reading his speeches in the final weeks, it was only because he finally chose to heed long-ignored advice. Only those closest to him saw the upset coming.

Trump in his Book "The Art of the Deal (1987) said "I like thinking big. I always have. To me its very simple: If you are going to be thinking anyway, you may as well think big. Most people think small, because most people are afraid of success, afraid of making decisions, afraid of winning."

One has to note that, when Trump shot from the lip, the mechanics of building a campaign fell on others to figure out. According to one American Journal, the 15th floor office of Trump Tower was filled by young staffers, many of whom had never worked on a House race, let alone a Presidential

---

[9] Ibid.

Bid. Trump clinched the GOP nomination on May 3, 2016, on that day he had no machine to drive his message. The frugal selected campaign had fewer than 75 staff members, no field program or data operation and a meagre fund raising team. But the Republican National Committee was ready to back him.

Ms. Katie Walsh, the Republican National Coalition (RNC) Chief of Staff, said the entire IT aspect of the Campaign including Facebook Advertisements, paid TV ads, phone calls, door knocks, cable news, newspaper ads, etc. were all managed by Mr. Brad Parscale, an expert Web Designer who had experience of working with Trump Companies, managed to reach voters in the distant areas across the United States.

According to a State Department Official in Washington, even RNC own Party model could not predict Trump's victory. The candidate Trump won several States with hands down and Mr. Brad Parscale's prediction came accurate and Trump was declared the Victor. Victory brings a happy challenge of huge proportions. Trump was declared President Elect on November 8, 2016 and Mr. Michael Pence, the Vice President.

Source: http://alajadi.com/donald-trump-win-us-presidential-elections/

THE NEW HOUSE

435 seats up for grabs
Republicans held the House with ease,
while Democrats were on course to pick
up just a handful of seats, far fewer than
the party once hoped.

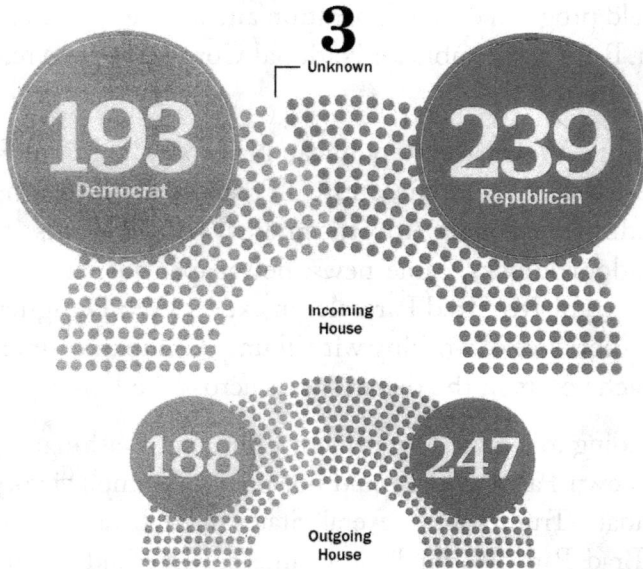

3
Unknown

193 Democrat

239 Republican

Incoming House

188

247

Outgoing House

Source: American Library, New Delhi

The above figure reflect the results of the US Elections and explain how America voted electorally. Hillary Clinton amassed nearly 66 million votes in the election-nearly 3 million more than Trump—the largest total for a losing candidate. However Trump garnered 279 electoral votes as against Clinton's 228 electoral votes and this made the difference.

Trump in the Oval Office—White House

Several Articles and reports from well-known magazines and newspapers such as Economist, Time Magazine and New York Times and the reports of Forbes and CSIS Washington have analyzed Trump's policies after his taking over Presidential seat.

Source: US Consulate General

Mr. Donald Trump took over as the 45th President of the United States on January 20, 2017. Mr. David Von Drehle, the well-known Feature Editor of the TIME Magazine wrote "The inauguration of a new President is always a balance between national legacy and the promise for a fresh start. It is common for a Speaker to try to set himself apart. Nevertheless, when Donald Trump stood for the first time as the 45th President of the United States, in a light rain to deliver his address, he went where no President had gone in more than a century. In 26 mostly harsh, mostly confrontational minutes, Trump laid out a view of America's destiny and a place in a World that would alienate his predecessors dating back to Theodore Roosevelt and beyond."

President Trump's Inaugural Speech

Sworn into Office as the 45th President, Trump delivered his inaugural speech announcing a U-turn in the US Foreign Policy that has defined America's place in the World for more than 70 years. TV coverage and Press Reports showed that he savaged the record and motives of a large number of men and women seated around him on the west front of the Capitol Hill. His choice of Vice President Mike Pence and his Cabinet appointments have been sharply conservative. Trump's first message to the World was as radical as they come and as populist as a pitchfork. The World is in for some big and unpredictable changes.

In his speech Trump said, American Power is a mirage. What happens abroad is a distraction from what matters at home. The US should work with suspicion, not pride, on the success of its Allies and trading partners. In a zero sum World, we either win or lose. "For many decades, we have enriched foreign industry as the expense of American Industry. Subsidized the army of other countries while allowing for the very sad depletion of our military" said Trump as rain began to fall in Washington. He added "we have defended other nations borders while refusing to defend our own and spent trillions and trillions of dollars overseas while America's infrastructure has fallen into disrepair and decay."[10]

"We have made other countries rich while the wealth, strength and confidence of our country has dissipated over the horizon". Trump summed up "from this day onwards, a new vision will govern our land. From this day forward, it's going to be only AMERICA FIRST". Diverting from his prepared speech he repeated the phrase: AMERICA FIRST.

The CNN TV Cameraman while covering the above event focused on Trump's fans assembled in thousands. Trump's speech was sweet music to his fans. "He is here to support us and help to be better" said one person in the crowd. Little later Trump stepped out of the rain to celebrate the gala lunch in Statuary Hall. In response to a toast Trump said "whether you are a Republican or a Democrat, does not make any difference. We are going to get along."

Commenting on the above developments, Mr. Ramesh Babu, former Professor of Political Science in Mumbai University said that the inaugural ceremony reminds us that our elections not wars, they are intra-squad scrimmages. Only during the fag end of the speech, Trump gestured towards unity. "When you open your hearts to patriotism, there is no room for prejudice." Trump declared "The Bible tells us, how good and pleasant it is when God's people live together in Unity. We must speak our minds openly, debate our disagreements honestly but always pursue solidarity." He added "when America is united, America is totally unstoppable.

---

[10] President's Inaugural Speech; USIS Library with photographs and Library of Congress Reports.
    Collection of Inaugural Speeches of Presidents, Washington DC.

From the Speech of President Trump, it appeared that he was promising to bring his much wanted private sector experience in conducting public sphere operations. Some of the intellectuals have started thinking how can lessons from business—from real estate deal making to large scale corporate management—apply to the work of government? Trump has been consistent in bringing a private sector sensibility to Washington. If one takes a look at his Cabinet, it is a group of billionaire business people such as Rex Tillerson, Secretary of State; Steve Mnuchin as Treasury Secretary; and Wilbur Ross as Commerce Secretary.

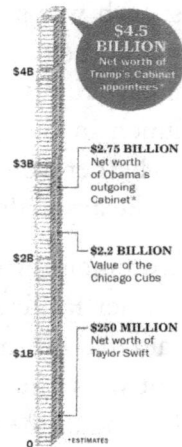

Trump's gilded team

Donald Trump has nominated the richest Cabinet and inner circle in modern U.S. history. The group has more wealth than the poorest one-third of U.S. households combined.
—*Abigail Abrams*

NET WORTH: $ 2.5 BILLION
WILBUR ROSS
Commerce
The "king of bankruptcy" made his fortune acquiring and restructuring failing companies

$1.25 BILLION
BETSY DEVOS
Education
After marrying an heir to the Amway fortune, DeVos became a conservative education activist

$3.25 MILLION
REX TILLERSON
State
As the CEO of ExxonMobil, he presided over millions in campaign donations and lobbying spending

$3.00 MILLION
STEVE MNUCHIN
Treasury
A former Goldman Sachs partner, he ran a bank that foreclosed on thousands of people during the recession

$45 MILLION
ANDY PUZDER
Labor
The fast food magnate could use his post to push back on policies like minimum-wage increases

$29 MILLION
BEN CARSON
Housing and Urban Development
The retired neurosurgeon has never held elected office and ran against Trump last year

$24 MILLION
ELAINE CHAO
Transportation
The former Labor Secretary is married to Senate majority leader Mitch McConnell and sits on four corporate boards

$10 MILLION
TOM PRICE
Health and Human Services
The Georgia Congressman invested in drug companies before co-sponsoring legislation that benefited them

$4.5 BILLION
Net worth of Trump's Cabinet appointees*

$4B

$2.75 BILLION
Net worth of Obama's outgoing Cabinet*
$3B

$2.2 BILLION
Value of the Chicago Cubs
$2B

$250 MILLION
Net worth of Taylor Swift
$1B

0

*ESTIMATES

Source: Bloomberg, American Library, New Delhi

All this is fine if Government can be run like a company which in fact was the premise of President Trump's electoral campaign "America ought to be run as a business and as a successful businessman he is suited to lead the charge."[11]

---

[11] SilpaKovvali,https://www.bostonglobe.com/opinion/2016/05/01/donald-you-can-run-government-like-business/wjNaom7pyS7 WavlB7muUrN/story.html, 02/05/2016 (accessed on 21/4/2017).
Jon Meacham, "Do Business Leaders Make Good Presidents?" http://time.com/4640173/business-leaders-good-presidents/ (accessed on 21/04/17).

A former Deputy Secretary of State said that experience of running large complicated Companies is valuable preparation for the large, complicated departments of governments. Late President Dwight Eisenhower (Ike) was the last President to display a fondness for big businessmen like Trump, Ike had preference for corporate types so much so that his first Cabinet which took office in 1953, was referred to as "Eight Millionaires and a Plumber". The Labor Secretary, then Mr. Martin Durkin, a Union Leader, was referred as Plumber. Eisenhower wrote in his diary that if successful industrialists are not included in the Cabinet, this will result in Government's inability to get anybody to take jobs in Washington except business failures, political hacks and new deal lawyers.

Under Trump's Presidency, US seems to look at the world very differently. Trump's nationalist stature perceives a different role for US in present international order. The pre-election proclamations of Trump and the post-election action are found to be totally opposite. There are several examples such as US relations with Russia, US stand regarding Syrian problem as well as about the role of NATO. Even his trade policies might follow the same path. Initially he may appear to be in favour of closing the doors of America, eventually the trade policy may once again take a liberal turn. So currently there is no much to worry about India-US relations.

CHAPTER 2

The Early Footsteps– Reviewing India-US Economic Engagement

The new chapter in the relationship between India and US said to have begun in the new millennium, when the two "estranged democracies" moved on the path of becoming "natural allies". The attempts to rebalance India's relationship with US began by Prime Minister Indira Gandhi in 1980 and furthered by Prime Minister Rajiv Gandhi in the late 1980s. Some of the dominant themes in India's contemporary relations with the US—from IT business connections to defence cooperation—can all be traced back to the Rajiv year's.[13] However political constraints of 'yet to over' cold war on the one hand, and the absence of outward looking foreign policy of India, the idea of strategic relationship did not prosper. Indian foreign policy till the end of cold war more or less followed Nehruvian idealism, accordingly economic considerations never got a priority over other considerations in foreign policy decision making. India intentionally avoided building closer relations with US during the cold war period. The end of cold war forced shift in India's foreign policy. The shift from bipolar world to unipolar world led by US on the

---

[13] C. Raja Mohan, "Modi's American Engagement" Http://www.India Seminar.com/2015/668/668_C_Raja_Mohan.Htm accessed on 7th June 2016.

one hand and economic downfall at home on the other hand forced Indian foreign policy become economically realistic.[14] To be more specific, massive change in the world politics and India's domestic economic compulsions almost forced India to adopt economic reforms in 1991 which started paying dividends in the new millennium.

The first and foremost challenge before India was to repay the huge debts. For the development of economy great amount of investment was required in infrastructure. And in the changed world conditions, US was considered to be one of the helping hand. India felt obliged to develop closer relations with US. However, India's positive moves of welcoming foreign direct investment did not attract the United States immediately. In the new world order, US was expected to play a major role. India was looked as a potential power but neither a major power, nor a preferred partner due to weak economy and mounting political and social problems. US tried to monopolise the economic and military power in the new world order that came into existence in the post-cold war period. During this phase, US did not perceive India as its economic partner, rather, it was interested in China which had already established itself as a major economic power by 1993. During this period, US interest in India was limited with respect to its non-proliferation drive in South Asia. US also threatened India to impose economic sanctions, if India would go ahead with the nuclear tests. As a result of its toughened stand and from India's perspective discriminatory stand on the issue of nuclear non-proliferation, the continuous

---

[14] Nandy, Debasish. "Indo-Usa Economic and Techno-Logical Cooperation: The Post Cold-War Scenario (1991-2006)." Journal of South Asian Studies 3.1 (2015): 61-75, accessed on 7th June 2016.

neglect of US regarding India's complaints of cross-border terrorism emanating from Pakistan and US-Pakistan-China axis, the relationship between India and US did not progress in the early decade of 90s.

Though India-US relations were not very positive, India had adopted the policy of "Look East" in order to build up strong economic links with the developed economies of South East Asia. Also India concentrated its attention on nations of Middle East in order to serve its energy needs. The policy of liberalization, brought Foreign Direct Investment, due to which Indian economy began to grow gradually. Growth in Indian economy changed US perceptions to a great extent. US realised that India has a tremendous long term economic potential in which US can have a significant share. US began to invest in the core sector of the economy such as hydrocarbon, electronics, computers etc. Before India launched economic reforms in 1991, US private sector investment in India was $19 million. By mid 1990s, it rose to $500 million and in the later period, up to $3.5 billion per year.[15] US multinationals such as Enron, Cogentrix began to invest into energy sector in India. The Indo-US economic cooperation was also extended in the areas like IT, Telecom Sector, pharmaceuticals, biotechnology, etc.

The Clinton Administration—"India is a major player in the economic field. The economic liberalisation policy of the Government of India has now paved the way for unprecedented trade and investment between India and the US."(http://www.idsa-india.org/an-jun-6.html)

---

[15] Ibid.

Evolution of India's Investment Regime[16]

Period	Liberalisation measures
Pre-1991	• The licensing system, governed by the Industries (Development and Regulation) Act of 1951, allowed the government to regulate investment decisions
1991-96	• Approval of 51% foreign ownership in 35 priority sectors, which was further expanded to 111 industries, with equity ownership limits upto 50%, 51%, 74% and 100%[43]
	• Removal of general ceiling of 40% under the Foreign Exchange Regulation Ac (FERA) on foreign ownership in FDI projects[44]
	• Sectors reserved for Small Sector Industries (SSI) were opened up for foreign investment upto 24% of equity ownership
1997-99	• Foreign Investment Promotion Board (FIPB) was set up to provide single-window clearance for FDI projects not under automatic approval
2000-05	• Consistent with its WTO-TRIMs commitments, dividend-balancing requirements were abolished for foreign investors by 2000; the indigenisation requirement in 2001; and the trade balancing requirement in 2002[45]
	• Foreign Exchange Management Act (FEMA) was introduced in 2000, which broadened the scope of FDI outflows
	• FDI up to 100 per cent under the automatic route in construction activities subject to some guidelines[46]
2006-09	• FDI allowed up to 100% in most activities/sectors[47]
	• Progressive liberalisation of the FDI policy regime, and simplification of procedures[48]
	• Liberaliation of FDI policies in sectors such as telecom, retail[49]
	• Expansion of coverage of FDI to credit information companies and commodity exchanges; widening access of foreign firms to local equity markets[50]
2010 - Sept. '12	• In November 2011, the government notified 51% FDI in multi-brand retail but later stalled implementation.[51] This pause was lifted in September 2012, with caveats
	• In January 2012, 100% FDI was allowed in single-brand retail [52]

Though, India-US relationship was appeared to be moving positively, nuclear tests of India in 1998, severely strained the relationship between the two. US imposed economic sanctions on India but it did not affect India's economy to a greater extent. India's ability to survive despite economic sanctions, forced US to think about India more seriously. As Indian economy began to grow, US also realised that India can offer enormous export and opportunities and started considering India more seriously. The possibilities of potential mutual gains created the environment for cooperation further leading to deepening of commercial ties. The US approach towards India started changing after

---

[16] HK Singh, "BIT and Beyond—Advancing India-US Economic Relations" icrier.org/pdf/bit and beyond.pdf, accessed on 9/9/2016.

the nuclear tests of 1998. After Pr. Clinton's visit to India in March 2000, followed by PM. Vajpayee's visit to US in September 2000 India-US bilateral relations took a new turn. US acknowledged India as an emerging economic and political partner and the global player. There were several economic achievements of this visit:

1. The US economic assistance to India was resumed which was stalled after the nuclear tests of 1998

2. Agreement for development of two thermal and one hydro power plant

3. Agreement to double bilateral trade—$15 billion in 3 years and increasing US investment in India—$15 billion per year

4. US assistance of $900 million to State Bank of India and to Exim Bank for purchase of US goods and services by Indian business.

It was accepted by both, that, they have mutual and complementary interests in different areas such as technology, energy, health, medicine, and defense and there is a high possibility that both can promote further exports, partnerships, collaboration, and joint innovation.

The New Millennium

The real recasting of the relationship between India and US began in the new millennium when US began to look at India from the strategic perspective—India as a balancer in the Asian Balance of Power. This resulted in changing the longstanding US apprehensions about India's nuclear capabilities. US took a clear stand of non-interference in Kashmir issue and was willing to treat India and Pakistan separately. This new thinking in US resulted in two important developments. There was an agreement over expanding defence cooperation between two countries and cooperation on combatting international terrorism. In keeping with the intention of developing a strategic partnership with India, US and India entered into an agreement—"Next Step in Strategic Partnership" in January, 2004. Both the countries agreed to extend cooperation in the areas of civilian nuclear technology, space exploration, missile defence, and high technology trade.

visual **EDIT** — [NF]news**flicks** To download our visual news app, just sms NF to 52424

15 years > than 52 in Indo-US relations

Beyond all the agreements, investment and trade, there is one simple and strong proof of the world's largest and oldest democracies coming closer than ever —US presidents now come every 4 years, versus every 14 in the past

1947-1999:	52 years			NUMBER OF US PRESIDENTIAL VISITS
	Dwight D. Eisenhower 1959	Richard Nixon 1969	Jimmy Carter 1978	3 visits
2000-2015:	15 years			
	Bill Clinton 2000	George W Bush 2006	Obama 2010, 2015	4 visits

Refer footnote 17

US trade with India multiplied over the last decade, with exports ranging from mining equipment and fertilizers, to steam and gas turbines and C-17 military aircraft. The United States is India's top investor and, as a group, Indian firms are among the fastest-growing investors in the US economy and have contributed jobs, innovation, and support to

---

[17] Visual Edit: 15 years beats 52 in Indo-US relations http://www.dailymail.co.uk/indiahome/indianews/article-2925933/VISUAL-EDIT-15-years-beats-52-Indo-relations.html#ixzz43YIMtG7X accessed on 21 December 2015.

communities throughout the United States. It is exciting and encouraging to see the energy, creativity, and dynamism of Indian firms taking root in and enriching the US economy.[18] In the last ten years, India-US relationship has developed into a global strategic partnership, based on increasing convergence of interests on bilateral, regional and global issues.[19] The bilateral relationship is getting strengthened due to cooperation in multiple sectors that include trade and investment, defence and security, science and technology, clean energy and environment, agriculture and health and education.

The further landmark development was Bush Administration's decision to pursue nuclear energy deal with India. India was technically ineligible for such deal as it had not signed NPT neither it had acceded to IAEA safeguards. In spite of this, it was Pr. Bush personal interest in India-US reapproachment which proved to be instrumental for this deal.

These agreements by America were based on its own assessment that, by 2025 India would be one of the world's five largest economies, having an enormous pool of highly educated and young people which would establish India as a force to reckon with in the 21st century.[20] The nuclear deal introduced in 2005 was approved by the Nuclear Suppliers Group in 2008. It was for the first time that US took initiative to facilitate India's access to nuclear fuel and technology.

---

[18] By Sonia Luthra, Deepening US-India Economic Engagement, An Interview with Ambassador Susan Esserman September 27, 2011http://www.nbr.org/research/activity.aspx?id=176 accessed on 21 December 2015.

[19] http://www.mea.gov.in/Portal/ForeignRelation/India-US_Relations.pdf

[20] Shukla, Subhash. Foreign policy of India. Anamika Pub & Distributors, 2007 page 261, accessed on 21 December 2015.

The major contentious issue remained was India's decision to restrict American Company's entry into India's Civil Nuclear Sector. But with all hindrances, the leadership of both the nations, PM. Dr. Manmohan Singh and President Bush made a headway to forge a strategic partnership in later half of 2008.

2008 financial crisis and recession, had an adverse effect on global trade of US. Even the bilateral trade between India and US declined by 15%.[21] India was only the United States' twelfth-largest trading partner, accounting for just 1.5% of America's total exports in 2010.[22]

Fragile Relations

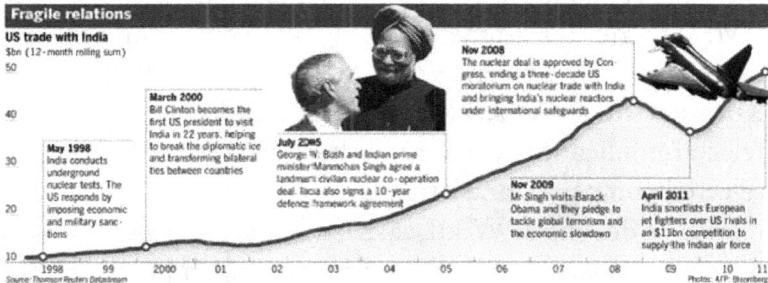

Refer footnote 23

The period from 2009 to 2014 can be said to be a period of sluggishness between India and US relationship. While, there were no specific issues that led to the stagnant relationship, there were several irritants, that, raised doubts about the potential of India-US strategic partnership. The issues ranged

---

[21] Ibid.

[22] Ibid.

[23] US lobbying fails to mask fighters' flaws, http://www.ft.com/intl/cms/s/0/9bb9dc06-7197-11e0-9b7a-00144feabdc0.html#axzz43XIMdr3V accessed on 4 June 2016.

from US decision to impose sanctions on Iran to India's decision to buy French (rather than American) aircraft estimated at US\$ 11 billion order for advance Fighters and Indian Parliaments' passage of legislation in August 2010 (Civil Liability for Nuclear Damage Bill) which virtually shut American companies out of India's Civil Nuclear Industry. The domestic challenges in both the nations, such as depressed economy of US, record high unemployment levels, budget deficits and the US Government's criticism of the practice of business outsourcing to India and other countries (which grew more pronounced as the 2012 Presidential election approached) on the one hand and left wing opposition to Indo-US nuclear deal on the other, continued to remain a major stress in the relationship. Further, PM. Singh's government faced the corruption charges especially with reference to a former Telecommunication Minister Mr. A. Raja, who allegedly sold second generation telecommunication licenses at less than market value to selected companies and other corruption scandals. Also, the release of dozens of WikiLeaks Cables dealing in US-India relations embarrassed the Government which prevented the government from taking any strong step for improving US-India relation.

Positive Turn in the Relationship

After the elections of 2012, there was a major change in the US Strategic designs. The decision to withdraw from Afghanistan, once again made US less sensitive to Pakistan's regional significance and at the same time there was a growing realization to respect India's strategic objectives and its efforts to rebuild Afghanistan.

After 2014 elections Prime Minister Modi's leadership seems to have brought a new warmth in the relationship between India and US. The change in the Indian perception of US and the realization of the role, US can play in India's global engagement has altered the dynamics of bilateral relationship between India and US. There is a significant change in India's foreign policy orientations which is indicated by the fact that India has adopted pro-active policy in its external relationships especially in its relations with US. US also began to exhibit growing interest in engaging with India.

Between June and August 2014, close to 6 top ranking officials from the US State Department, US Department of Commerce and Department of Defence visited New Delhi. Mr. John Kerry, US Secretary of State and Commerce Secretary and Ms. Penny Pritzger visited India on July 30 and 31st for participating in the 5th Annual India-US Strategic Dialogue held in New Delhi. The Indian side was led by Foreign Minister Ms. Sushma Swaraj and her team of officials including Nirmala Sitaraman, Minister of State for Commerce and Industry. After Prime Minister Modi's visit to Washington during September 2014, several steps such as meeting of the Counter Terrorism Joint Working Group, Ministerial level Home and Security and Trade Policy Forum dialogues, the CEO Forums and High Technology Co-operation Group and US participation in India's Annual Technology Summit in November 2014 laid the strong foundations for US-India economic engagement.

"Both India and USA are global engines of growth. Trade, commerce and investment are key areas. Technology, innovation and knowledge economy are also areas were are actively looking at." (http://indianexpress.com/article/india/both-india-and-usa-are-global-engines-of-growth-top-quotes-from-pm-modis-presser-with-donald-trump-4723644/)

BIG ISSUES ON AGENDA

CLIMATE CHANGE
US may seek India's backing for global climate deal slated for Paris at the end of the year. But agreement akin to the US-China one, when Beijing agreed to cap carbon emissions, unlikely

INDO-US CIVIL-NUCLEAR AGREEMENT
Breakthrough in talks over civil nuclear liability, stuck since 2008

DEFENCE & SECURITY TIES
Decade-old defence cooperation pact, expiring this year, may be renewed. Delhi is the world's largest buyer of US weapons, importing arms worth $6 billion every year

ECONOMIC TIES
Concentration likely on trade and investments, much dialogue to centre on how Washington can help Modi deliver on promise to boost India's economy

WHERE INDIA STANDS

➤ India **world's third-largest economy** by purchasing power ranks only 11th-largest goods trading partner with the US

➤ It's the **18th-largest destination** for US exports

➤ In 2013, trade between the two countries amounted to **$93 billion**

➤ Since 2000, cumulative FDI from US into India only about **$12.7 billion** — less than that from Singapore, the UK, the Netherlands and even United Arab Emirates

Refer footnote 24

The outstanding issues in their bilateral relationship—the implementation of Civil Nuclear Initiative, concerns over

---

[24] http://timesofindia.indiatimes.com/india/Obama-visit-India-United-States-close-to-breaking-nuclear-deal-deadlock/articleshow/46006662.cms accessed on 4 June 2016

India's membership of Nuclear Suppliers Group, cooperation over Climate Change policies expanding the use of renewable energy in the total energy consumption are on the verge of resolution. The Joint Vision Statement on Indian Ocean and India-Pacific region can be sighted as the example of breakthrough understanding between India and US. This also laid down the strong foundation for enriched diplomatic, security and economic relationship.

Bilateral Investment Treaty

India and US seem to have realised, that, to deal with global economic uncertainty, there is need to increase collaboration in common interest areas. The United States and India each have a stake in the other's economic well-being and ensuring a strong recovery. The negotiation of a bilateral investment treaty (BIT) would be an important step to addressing barriers to investment and would promote the rule of law and stability at a time of great uncertainty in the global economic environment. In view of US policy makers, Bilateral Investment Treaty is the foundation for its agreements on investor protection and to promote two way economic partnership with other countries.

In 2008, the initial talks on the Bilateral Investment Treaty (BIT) began between India and US. The purpose was to provide for the legal framework and rules that will regulate US investments in India and Indian investments in US. The formal negotiations regarding BIT commenced in August 2009. The 'Framework for Cooperation on Trade and Investment' signed between both the countries reaffirmed that, "The United States and India recognize that each benefits from the other's success in expanding economic opportunity, creating jobs, reducing poverty, and enhancing the wellbeing of its citizens.[25]

Why US Interest in BIT

US interest in Bilateral Investment Treaty reaffirms that US perception of India has changed. US has begun to perceive India as an important trade and investment partner, though currently it is only the 13th largest trade partner of US[26]. US therefore believes that India's potential is far from being used. This US perception is the result of India's consistency in economic growth and the prediction that India is on the way of becoming world's 3rd largest economy. Though, US-India trade relations have improved significantly after 2005, after the economic recession in US and several other strains at the domestic level in both US and India, the share of Indian trade that involves US and US share of total Foreign Direct Investment in India, both began to decline. US is also aware that India is engaged in trade relationship with many other countries including major nations in European Union, ASEAN, Japan and South Korea. If there is no concrete development in India-US relations, India may have to turn to other economic partners which is not in the interest of US. BIT therefore is important for a forward movement in India-US relationship. It is believed that it will strengthen India-US trade relations, help protect and promote investments and guarantee international minimum standards in the treatment of foreign investments. BIT

---

[25] Mili Saxena*, Dr. Padmini Ravindra Nath* Global Economic Recession and its implications for Indo-US Trade http://jaipuria.edu.in/pgdm/wp-content/uploads/2013/11/Paper-7.pdf accessed on 4 June 2016.

[26] Matthew Stokes and Niraj Patel, BIT and Beyond Advancing the US-India economic relationship, A report of the CSIS Wadhwani Chair in US-India policy studies, accessed on 4 June 2016.

will be beneficial for both nations as the private sectors of India and US will have a freedom to enter into other's market. It will serve India's need for much needed FDI and also create job opportunities in both the nations and build the stronger ties.

Complications in BIT

There is no agreement between India and US over the preconditions set by India. The major US objection is regarding India's insistence that the commercial disputes that may arise in foreign investments will be decided according to the verdict of Indian courts and the investors will not have a right to invoke international dispute settlement measures. India does not agree to Investor State Dispute Settlement under which investors can refer the disputes regarding treaty obligations to international arbitration tribunal. India insists that, such disputes should be brought first before the local judicial and administrative authorities and after all such means are exhausted, they can be referred to international tribunal. Also international tribunals cannot re-examine any issue that is settled by the judicial authority of the host country.

In fact, Provision for a dispute settlement procedure as a part of treaty is a most general practice which is in consent with international arbitration by a tribunal. This provision is advantageous because it is a guarantee that the disputes relating to investments will be resolved by qualified tribunal and therefore there is a good possibility of fair judgement. However, Indian fear is that if the disputes relating to investments are referred to the third party tribunal, it may not understand the local problems created by investors. Generally, such tribunals favour investors, and therefore the disputes settlement might always go in favour of US.

Also, there is a vast difference in the Indian model of BIT and US model of BIT in the sense of US definition of investment and Indian definition of investment. For US, investment includes, business enterprises, shares, bonds, debentures, derivatives, intellectual property rights, business concessions, contractual rights, and moveable and immovable property which is quite broad-based. For India, Investment is confined to only FDI in the host state and not portfolio investments, government debt securities, commercial contracts, goodwill and other intangible assets of an enterprise. Further, the investors who directly own and control an enterprise and have real and substantial business operations, long-term capital investment and large number of employees in the host State will only be covered by the Treaty. It implies that small business enterprises or indirect and minority shareholders, will not be protected by the Treaty. Also the Indian model of BIT, does not accept the condition of granting US, the MFN status, which will prevent the US investors from invoking more favourable substantive protection standards contained in India's other BITs.

Another bone of contention is, US demand that the investment terms for US investors should be similar to the Indian investors. That means, India cannot impose performance requirements on US enterprises as a condition of investment. Whereas in India's BIT with other nations, there is a provision that, India maintains the right to screen foreign investors prior to their establishing an investment presence in the country and guarantees post establishment equal treatment.

US investors felt that such conditions hamper their interests and thus create unfavourable climate for bilateral investment.

As a result, the multinationals started pulling out from Indian markets. That put Foreign Direct Investment came under fragile conditions. Meanwhile, Indian investments in the United States have risen from US$200 million to US$5 billion between 2000 and 2010, and further rose to US$11 billion in 2012. This led to a mentionable growth in the US economy and created more than 100,000 jobs. Similar results were likely to appear in India had the government taken swift, proactive steps to facilitate foreign investments and provide Indian investors with incentives to invest in domestic projects.[27]

The US model contains detailed provisions on environment and labour standards. India has always opposed such standards in bilateral agreements and at the WTO. It remains to be seen whether India will accept these provisions under the proposed India-US BIT. The Indian model deals only with disclosure and anti-corruption provisions.

It is also uncertain, whether, the US will agree to India's proposal to keep intellectual property rights (including compulsory licenses), taxation matters, and measures taken to ensure financial and macroeconomic stability outside the framework of the proposed treaty. [28]

---

[27] Ashish Goel, King's College London, and Harish Goel, XLRI. "India-US bilateral investment treaty going nowhere" East Asia Forum | August 31st, 2013, http://www.bilaterals.org/?india-us-bilateral-investment&lang=fr accessed on 4 June 2016.

[28] Kavaljit Singh, Madhyam. "The India-US Bilateral Investment Treaty will not be an easy ride" 10 February 2015, http://www.eastasiaforum.org/2015/02/10/the-india-us-bilateral-investment-treaty-will-not-be-an-easy-ride/ accessed on 11 July 2016.

INVESTMENT PACT PROVES ELUSIVE

Arbitration scope

- India says international arbitration last resort after all legal remedies at home have been exhausted
- US has also objected to clause that blocks India from being dragged in tax-related cases

Procurement access

- India doesn't want treaty to cover govt orders; benefits and grants to be only for Indian firms
- US wants most-favoured treatment for its investors

Environment watch

- India doesn't want US to bring in its own labour & environment norms

Rights reserved

- India hesitant to bring IPR within the ambit of treaty

Refer footnote 29

According to US, though, there is a lot of talk on BIT, the progress will be slow due to slow pace of economic reforms in India. Undersecretary of Commerce for International Trade at the US Department of Commerce Stefan Selig said during a discussion organised by the Council on Foreign Relations, "The BIT will be great for US companies in terms of their ability to invest in India. Frankly it will be even better for India because it will gradually create a framework for economic growth within the country. It is one of those perfect win-win opportunities if we are able to get there in terms of the high-standard agreement".[30]

---

[29] "Modi set for US, sans key treaty" http://www.telegraphindia.com/1150921/jsp/business/story_43632.jsp#.VvAlb_I942w accessed on 11 July 2016.

[30] "India must ensure economic reforms for progress on bilateral investment treaty: US", The Economic Times, Sep 16, 2015 http://articles.economictimes.indiatimes.com/2015-09-16/news/66604810_1_bilateral-investment-treaty-us-india-strategic-progress accessed on 11 September 2016.

PATH TO A PARTNERSHIP

HOW LAST 15 YEARS OF INDO-US TIES PANNED OUT

2000

Bill Clinton visits India, the first US presidential trip since 1978. First step to improve ties after 1998 N-sanctions. In Sept, Clinton hosted A B Vajpayee at largest state dinner of his presidency

George Bush sends deputy state secretary **Richard Armitage** to Delhi as special emissary. Bush declares strategic partnership with India and removes all remaining sanctions that were removed in 1999

2001

2004

India, US announce steps in partnership initiatives in civilian N-activities & space tech. US declares Pak 'major non-Nato ally'. New Delhi annoyed

Secy of state Condoleezza Rice visits Delhi. Starts dialogue on energy security. Upswing in ties despite tensions over India's possible energy cooperation with Iran and US sale of F-16s to Pak. India, US sign defence framework. India, US ink Civil N-cooperation Initiative that lifts 3-decade US moratorium on nuclear trade with India

2005

George W Bush visits India. N-deal signed with PM Manmohan Singh on civil nuclear cooperation

2006

2008

India buys 6 C-130J military planes. Bush signs law to enact US-India N-deal. After 26/11, FBI joins Indian investigations

2009

US announces it has arrested Headley & Rana. Singh & Obama meet in first state visit of his presidency. They launch 'knowledge initiative' to boost ties on education

India enacts law on civil liability for N-damage, strict provisions dampen prospects for civil N-cooperation. India, US sign anti-terror pact. On his India trip, Obama addresses Parliament, backs India for a permanent UN security council seat

2010

Obama suggests role for India in his 'Pivot To Asia' policy. India rejects bids by US cos seeking $12bn fighter jet contract

2011

Deepen defence cooperation, says US defence secretary Leon Panetta on India visit

2012

US complains in WTO against India's solar policy. Tensions as Devyani Khobragade arrested on charges of alleged visa fraud.

2013

US envoy Nancy Powell meets BJP's PM-candidate Modi, ending decade-old boycott. Ties put on mend with Obama's congratulatory call. John Kerry's India visit

2014

Refer footnote 31

---

[31] http://timesofindia.indiatimes.com/india/Obama-visit-India-United-States-close-to-breaking-nuclear-deal-deadlock/articleshow/46006662.cm accessed on 4 June 2016.

Institutionalization of Indo-US Economic Relations

At the institutional level, The American Chamber of Commerce in India (AMCHAM) and US India Business Council (USIBC), which is accredited to the Chamber of Commerce of USA is playing a vital role in consolidation of India-US economic engagement. The organization works for stimulating the investment of US companies in India, identifying opportunities for bilateral trade between the two, convince the Indian policy makers to bring reforms in the regulatory framework of business conditions that would help remove major obstacle in the trade relations and boost US investment in India. The organization is working seriously to improve the business climate in India by trying to remove major impediments such as unpredictable business environment, lack of clear governance norms, unambiguous policies and help the Indian Government to adopt a holistic approach to all sectors of investment, thereby help Indian economy back on the track.

President Obama's Historic Visit

* Strategic Dialogue elevated to 'Strategic & Commercial Dialogue' reflecting joint commitment to strengthening of commercial ties & promoting regional economic growth & stability.

* U.S. can offer new technology partnerships in the realms of energy, environment, defense, health care, education, etc to supercharge India's development trajectory.

* U.S. & India negotiating long-term energy supply arrangements that could boost India's energy security.

* Proposed LNG imports from US ~ 5.8 MTPA/US$2.5 billion from Sep 2017 from the terminal of Sabine Pass on the Louisiana-Texas border.

* Strengthening of Bilateral defense ties - joint manufacture of some equipment.

* US surpassed Russia as India's biggest arms supplier. US$ 5 billion worth of weapons procured from US (total $14b)

* India is now on par with NATO on the sophistication of defense technology offered to India.

* India conducts maximum defense exercises with USA.

Source: http://slideplayer.com/slide/4230680

US-India Strategic and Commercial Dialogue

In January 2015, to promote the commercial and economic partnership between US and India, PM Modi and Pr. Obama decided to establish the first-ever US-India Strategic and Commercial Dialogue—an annual forum for policy discussions between the United States Government and the Government of India. This move reflects a commitment of both US and India to strengthen the economic engagement that lies at the centre of bilateral relationship between the two. It includes business, education, cultural, familial and people-to-people ties that would lead the US-India partnership, and has a lot of scope to expand. Thereby, the forum would help advance shared priorities of generating economic growth, creating jobs and strengthening the middle class.

US-India CEO Forum

US-India CEO Forum was first constituted in 2005 at the initiative of PM Manmohan Singh and Pr. Bush when the relationship between India and US was on the verge of turning into strategic partnership. This initiative aimed at enhancing bilateral trade and investment between the two countries. It was one important example of public-private partnership at the international level, where 10 CEOS from each country were engaged in developing a road map for increasing partnership and cooperation between the two countries at the business level. The report of the CEO forum presented in 2006 was entitled as "US-India strategic economic partnership". The forum defined 6 priority initiatives—promotion of trade and industry, creation of infrastructure development fund, promote technology exchange in agriculture, Bio technology and Nano technology, partner in skill development set up an

Indo-US centre for Industrial R&D and establish a dispute resolution mechanism. The purpose of this forum is to bring together the leaders of respective business communities of US and India to discuss the issues of mutual interest and the ways to strengthen the economic and commercial ties between the two countries. In 2015 meet, The CEO Forum offered suggestions in key areas such as business climate, smart cities and infrastructure financing, supply chain integration (including cold chain), aerospace/defense, and renewable energy among other topics.

The US-India Commercial Dialogue

The Commercial Dialogue is also a forum of public-private partnership. The governments of both the countries and the private sector in India and US in which both governments and the Indian and US private sectors, American Chambers of commerce, the US-India Business council and the Federation of Indian Chambers of Commerce and Industry. They collaborate on issues of mutual interest, thereby ensuring that our trade relationship continues to grow and diversify. The US Department of Commerce and India's Ministry of Commerce and Industry have taken steps to renew the Commercial Dialogue for an additional two-year term until March 2016.

Trade Policy Forum

This forum primarily focuses on the policy issues that have an impact of bilateral trade and investment. The forum activities include the expert level and senior official discussions on intellectual property, manufacturing, services, and agriculture that will help advance cooperation on bilateral trade objectives.

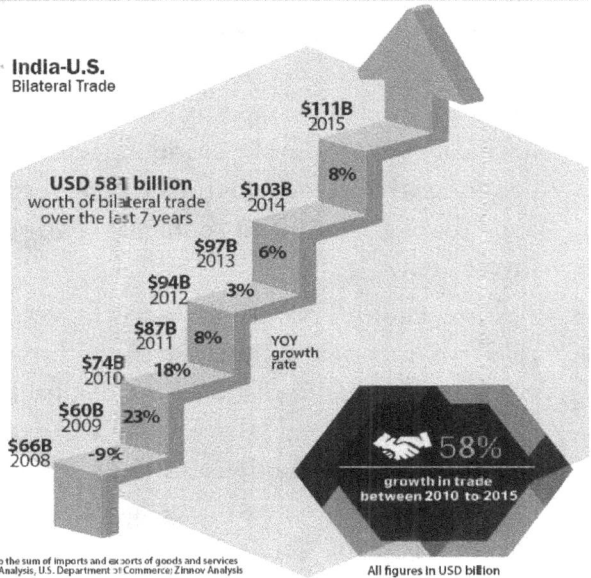

Source: *American Library, New Delhi; Asiatic Library, Mumbai*

Apart from the institutional mechanisms established to further and strengthen India-US economic relationship, there are several agreements between India and US and joint programmes which will be undertaken by the governments of both the nations which would help consolidation of their relationship. The prominent among them are:[32]

1. The initiative for ease of doing business that includes commercial law initiative to exchange best practices on matters like contract enforcement, insolvency and bankruptcy law, and cross border trade, including non-tariff barriers.

---

[32] US-India Commercial, Trade and Economic Cooperation—fact sheet http://www.state.gov/r/pa/prs/ps/2015/09/247174.htm accessed on 4 June 2016.

2. Collaboration on Cluster Mapping: This will help Indian companies integrate into global supply chains, strengthen India's economy and better enable American companies to identify markets for their products and services in India. Cluster mapping will help US and Indian decision-makers develop more effective, evidence-based commercial linkages that will drive economic growth and development and enhance two-way trade and investment.

3. An Innovation Forum—It is a private sector led forum to serve as an additional avenue through which our governments seek private sector feedback and input for bilateral discussions. The Forum will consider a set of rotating topics to ignite and scale innovation, increase related two-way investment and trade, support the advancement of small and medium-sized enterprises (SMEs), and identify where specific skill sets are needed to propel innovation forward.

4. Product and Reference Standards Cooperation: The United States and India are working together to participate in the development of international standards and technical regulations to boost trade and help reduce administrative and logistical burdens, which disproportionately affect small and medium sized enterprises.

5. Strengthening Best Practices in Manufacturing: The United States Department of Commerce's National Institute of Standards and Technology's Manufacturing Extension Partnership (NIST-MEP) will share best practices in manufacturing and supply chain integration. The NIST-MEP invited senior Indian officials to visit

the main NIST site in Gaithersburg, Maryland in October 2015.

6. Investment Promotion: The US Department of Commerce's Select USA initiative and the Silicon Valley chapter of The Indus Entrepreneurs (TiE) signed a memorandum of intent on September 18, 2015 to work together to provide Indian entrepreneurs the data and assistance they need to facilitate their expansion into the United States. Participation in the Americas Competitiveness Exchange (ACE) for Innovation and Entrepreneurship.

7. The United States has invited the Government of India to participate in the United States Department of Commerce's ACE program. Through ACE, senior Indian commercial and economic decision-makers have the ideal opportunity to establish long-term global and regional partnerships and to see the results of economic development initiatives in the Americas that are strengthening innovation and entrepreneurship ecosystems.

8. Information and Communication Technology Working Group: The United States and India held the first meeting of the US-India Information and Communication Technology Working Group where the US put forth a draft work plan to facilitate collaboration and development in support of Prime Minister Modi's "Digital India" initiative.

9. US-India Memorandum of Understanding on Agriculture: The United States Department of Agriculture (USDA) and the Indian Ministry of Agriculture plan to renew their now-expired Memorandum of Understanding (MOU). The scope of the renewed MOU will be expanded to

facilitate engagement on a broader and more inclusive range of topics than its predecessor.

10. US-India Agricultural Dialogue: The governments of India and the United States are evaluating the possibility for renewal of the Agricultural Dialogue. A reinvigorated Dialogue would include the broad scope of food and agricultural regulatory and policy setting agencies, and provide a mechanism for identifying shared opportunities and areas for cooperation.

11. Smart Cities Infrastructure Business Development Mission: The United States Department of Commerce's Deputy Secretary will lead a Trade Mission to further smart cities development in India, introduce US technologies and solutions to boost the energy efficiency of India's infrastructure, and support efforts to build the commercial relationship in sectors that contribute to shared environmental objectives. In advance of this mission, the Deputy Secretary of Commerce co-hosted an event with the Federation of Indian Chambers of Commerce and Industry and 32 Advisors on September 21 to foster collaboration between Indian and US businesses on specific infrastructure and smart cities opportunities. The Trade Mission visit took place on February 8-12, 2016.

12. Indian Smart Cities Participation in NIST Global Cities Teams Challenge 2.0: The United States invited the Government of India to participate in the next round of the Global City Teams Challenge (GCTC) organized by the United States Department of Commerce's US National Institute of Standards and Technology (NIST). The next round's objective is to encourage deployment

of technologies to show measurable quality-of-life improvements. The Challenge facilitates partnerships among: city and community planners and project managers to identify common issues, share solutions, and design new approaches; technology innovators and providers to integrate technologies and create standards-based platforms suitable for use across sectors such as energy, the environment, transportation, resilience, and health care; and scientists, engineers, and technologists to translate the results of smart city R&D into practice. Participants in the Challenge will also work together with other international counterparts in developing a smart city framework and standards and technology roadmaps for interoperability.

13. The US-India Infrastructure Collaboration Platform (ICP): The ICP is a cooperative, interagency effort between the United States and the Government of India, anchored by the United States Department of Commerce and the Indian Ministry of Finance and operated in concert with our two private sectors, to promote US private sector engagement in India's infrastructure growth and modernization. This effort develops business opportunities by matching unique US company capabilities with India's specific infrastructure needs, in areas such as power, transportation, water and sanitation, safety and security, and health care. The ICP was launched at a January meeting in Delhi. A second meeting took place in July 2015.

14. Invitation for Smart Cities Comprehensive Economic Development Strategy (CEDS) Program: The United States invited the Government of India to participate

in the CEDS program, administered through the United States Department of Commerce's Economic Development Administration. This program would initiate a regionally-owned planning process in India designed to build capacity and guide economic prosperity and resilience related to smart city and other projects. And it would provide a coordinating mechanism for individuals, organizations, clusters, local governments, and private industry.

15. Smart Solutions for Smart Cities Reverse Trade Mission: To further the partnership between the United States and India on smart cities development, the US Trade and Development Agency (USTDA) has invited a delegation of Andhra Pradesh and central government officials to the United States for a Smart Solutions for Smart Cities Reverse Trade Mission later this year. The visit will introduce the delegates to US technologies, solutions and best practices that can support the development of safe, efficient and integrated energy, transportation and communications urban infrastructure.

16. Technical Advisory Services for Smart City Development: The US Trade and Development Agency (USTDA) approved funding for technical specialty services to support smart city development in India. USTDA-funded experts in the fields of integrated urban and regional planning, as well as in energy, transportation and information communications technology infrastructure, will travel to India to provide advice and support to key stakeholders in advancing smart city planning and infrastructure development. The specialists will also identify and evaluate smart city project opportunities in India for USTDA funding consideration.

17. Increased Collaboration on Cold Chain and Supply Chain: The Public-Private Senior Executive Cold-Chain Roundtable was held in New Delhi in November 2015. The event will coincide with a large trade show in Chandigarh, India being organized by the Global Cold Chain Association, a major US trade association that represents cold chain equipment and supply chain management providers. Roundtable topics will include adopting operational best practices for cold chain storage and supply chain management processes; applying transportation and inventory management technology; and creating a more attractive environment for investment.

18. Indo-Pacific Economic Corridor (IPEC) Strategy: Complementing India's Enhanced Look East Policy, the United States envisions an Indo-Pacific Economic Corridor that can help bridge South and Southeast Asia—where the Indian and Pacific Oceans converge and where trade has thrived for centuries. Fostering these types of connections—physical infrastructure, regulatory trade architecture, and human and digital connectivity will create linkages all the way from Central Asia to Southeast Asia, via South Asia. A more integrated South Asia where markets, economies, and people connect is more likely to thrive and prosper. The United States is firmly committed to the security and prosperity of the Asian continent, and better connectivity, energy security, and stronger trade and investment links can help realize that objective. During the January 2015 visit, President Obama and Prime Minister Modi pledged to work together to increase connectivity across the Indian Ocean and Asia-Pacific Regions. IPEC operationalizes

this commitment, and the United States looks forward to implementing programs that support these objectives.

19. South Asia Regional Energy Law Cooperation: The US Department of Commerce's Commercial Law Development Program will partner with the Indian government to strengthen India's insolvency and procurement regimes and develop model contracts. This exchange is aimed at cultivating the investment regime in South Asia to attract more domestic, regional, and international capital for domestic and cross-border power projects. These activities fall under the broader US State Department Indo-Pacific Economic Corridor initiative to promote increased regional energy connectivity and contribute to the future development of a regional energy market in South Asia through cooperation, capacity building, and technical assistance.

20. US-India Transportation Partnership: The Department of Transportation and the Indian Ministry of Road Transport and Highways, and Shipping in April 2015 established the US-India Transportation Partnership. Comprised of the US Department of Transportation and the Indian Ministry of Road Transport and Highways, Shipping, and the Railways Ministry, the Transportation Partnership guides collaboration across a broad range of transport topics identified by a Joint Working Group. The inaugural meeting of the Joint Working Group took place in October 2015 in Washington, D.C. The topics included the transport elements of Smart Cities, Intelligent Transportation Systems, best practices for planning and funding transportation infrastructure projects, regional connectivity, and other areas of mutual interest.

21. Fifth US-India Aviation Summit: The US Trade and Development Agency (USTDA) and Government of India jointly hosted the 5th US-India Aviation Summit from November 3-5, 2015 in Bangalore, India. It was decided to establish collaboration under the US-India Aviation Cooperation Program (ACP) by offering high-level government and business aviation leaders the opportunity to set bilateral priorities, identify new high technology cooperation areas and build a larger commercial engagement agenda.

22. Aviation Security Equipment Testing and Evaluation Program: Supporting the two countries' interest to increase collaboration in the critical aviation security arena, the United States Trade and Development Agency (USTDA) is funding the first aviation security cooperation project under the US-India Aviation Cooperation Program (ACP). The technical assistance effort, also supported by the US Transportation Security Administration (TSA) and three member companies of the ACP, is designed to assist the Airports Authority of India (AAI) and India's Bureau of Civil Aviation Security (BCAS) to establish an Aviation Security Equipment Testing and Evaluation Program (ASETEP) to modernize India's aviation security environment in alignment with international standards and practices. The TA program will help India's civil aviation security authorities to develop clear standards for state-of-the-art aviation security equipment as well as build the technical capacity to test and certify needed systems that scan carry-on luggage, checked baggage and passengers. Under the program a delegation of Indian security officials will visit TSA testing labs in the US.

23. Advanced Passenger Screening Pilot Project: Working with US industry, the US Trade and Development Agency (USTDA) is sponsoring a pilot project to demonstrate the benefits of using advanced US airport passenger screening equipment at Delhi International Airport.

24. Rail Sector Development: The US Trade and Development Agency (USTDA) approved funding to support a leasing and public private partnership framework technical assistance project with India's Ministry of Railways. The project will advise the Ministry on how to modify its financing, procurement and operational policies for locomotives and other rail infrastructure projects, in order to mobilize private sector investment for the modernization of India's rail infrastructure.

Conclusion

In the US-India relationship, economic engagement remains at the top of the agenda for both sides. Economic co-operation has been the primary engine of closer relations, as Indian reforms have allowed a rapid expansion of US-India trade investment flows in both directions for the last 20 years. The progress made on economic ties has set the stage for successes in other phases of the relationship, such as military co-operation. However, now that co-operation in defence, education, and strategic issues is going stronger. A strong India-American community is playing a greater role in helping creating jobs in USA on the one hand and also shaping the American perceptions of India on the other. It is thus creating positive environment for potential India-US relations and building up the trust in the relations between the two. Both Governments recognize the key role that trade and investment play in this partnership and the Indian Government has made a promising return to its internal economic reform agenda. Both the Governments should now act with vision and determination to capitalize on this momentum and propel the US-India economic partnership forward.

CHAPTER 3

Strategic and Security Dimensions of India-US Relations

The relationship between India and US is officially described as "Strategic Partnership" which has grown significantly in the past decade. Strategic Partnership refers to an alignment or an alliance which shows specific characteristics. It can be described as cooperation among the nation states for mutual gains that includes maximising their own dominance and extending their spheres of influence. It also results in balancing their power positions in the international system. It follows that, the purpose of strategic partnership is not to target the policies against a particular hostile state but rather to focus on general security structure or responding to the international system. So the nations enter into partnership not because they have a common enemy to defeat—that is shared values in the negative sense, but they come together for common purpose—mutual interests of both the partners a more positive purpose. Thus, their alliance is not threat driven but goal driven and therefore equal importance is given to economic and trade relationship and security relationship or partnership. Though common security interests and strong military alliances are the part of the relationship, the relationship is build up on flexible terms rather than bound by rigid terms of treaty. As such agreement allows more freedom of operation for the members of alliance.

Former Indian Ambassadar to the US, Lalit Mansingh, suggests that for a strategic partnership to blossom, the presence of three factors is necessary: a) long-term vision, b) volume of exchange, c) defence and security pact or understanding. Chinese Prime Minister Wen Jiabao holds that a strategic partnership should take place on an "equal footing", should be long-term and mutually beneficial. Thomas Renard describes the following criteria based on which one can decide if a partnership is a strategic one. A strategic partnership: must be comprehensive so that there are linkages and trade-offs between various policies; must be built upon reciprocity; must have a strong empathic dimension (which means that both partners share a common understanding of their mutual values and objectives) and; must be on a long term basis, which is to say that, it is not put into question by casual disputes and must go beyond bilateral issues to tackle (or have the potential to solve) regional and global challenges.[33]

Understanding India-US "Strategic Partnership"

After decades of troubled relationship between India and US, the warming up of bilateral relationship began from 1990s, which has now culminated into healthy India-US relationship. India-US relations were first described as a

---

[33] Deba R. Mohanty & Uma Purushothaman, "India-US Defence Relations: In Search of a Direction" OBSERVER RESEARCH FOUNDATION, New Delhi, ORF OCCASIONAL PAPER #23 August 2011, accessed on 4 June 2016.
http://www.orfonline.org/cms/export/orfonline/modules/occasionalpaper/attachments/defence_1315307316072.pdf accessed on 4 June 2016.

strategic partnership in the Vajpayee-Bush joint statement of 2004, which called for the Next Steps in Strategic Partnership. Today both the countries cooperate in economic, strategic and diplomatic spheres. Leaders and policy-makers in both India and US believe, that, they share common goals and they are the important strategic partners. The relationship thus, confirms to the above description of "Strategic Partnership".

Refer footnote 34

[34]http://www.mapsofindia.com/my-india/government/why-hagel-is-here-will-talk-shop-and-more

The relationship between India and US was never so close and cozy, rather during cold war period, it was characterised by suspicion and bitterness. After India's independence, initially US perceived India an important ally for its central strategic needs. It was expected that India would serve as an important front in US cold war strategy—strategy of containment of global communism. So US supported India economically and militarily. But Indian intentions were clear. It was not ready to be partner either of US or USSR in the cold war context and defined its strategy as non-alignment. But due to India's adoption of Socialistic pattern of Society and the policy of state controlled economy, US began to perceive India as Soviet ally and doubted genuineness of India's non-alignment policy. The distrust that developed between US and India continued till the end of cold war.

After the end of cold war convergence of structural, domestic and individual leadership factors transformed Indo-US relations. By the time when cold war came to an end, it was proved to India that the socialist model of development did not prove successful and India needed market oriented reforms. As India moved towards market friendly economic policies, gradually India's economic performance began to improve. The GDP growth rate reached to almost 8.5% in the early years of new millennium from bare 3% in 1990s. India also emerged as a major player in the information technology sector and also an important source of skilled labour. The changes in Indian policies and approach was the result of not only its own needs in the changing times, but also, changes in the international system that were brought by the end of cold war. The international system changed from bipolar world to unipolar and then multipolar world that believed in cooperation among the nation-states, than mere power considerations and more flexible alignments than cold war rigid alignments. Along with the systemic changes, the political equations also began to change.

Changing Strategic and Political Equations

The strategic political equations of India and US started changing after the end of cold war and collapse of Soviet Union. During cold war period, US priorities never matched India's interests and policies, but the forces that kept India and US apart almost vanished with end of cold war and the common interests, which created prospects for positive India-US relationship emerged. Pakistan was a strategically important nation for US during the cold war to contain Soviet Union. After soviet withdrawal from Afghanistan and disintegration of Soviet Union, US abandoned both Afghanistan and its all-time ally Pakistan. In the Unipolar world, US was more concerned with the issue of nuclear proliferation in Asia. As India was unwilling to sign the Nuclear Non-proliferation Treaty despite continues US persuasion, the relations between the two remained strained. But at the same time, US imposed sanctions on Pakistan due to Pakistan's continued nuclear weapons programme. This decision signalled that US began to treat India and Pakistan equally. Though, it did not bring obvious benefits for India, it had a lot of significance for India. After the Soviet collapse, India did not have a reliable ally in the global politics. Continued US-Pakistan equation would have worsened the security scenario for India. The declining interest of US in Pakistan, therefore, was seen as a positive development for India.

In the new global system, when India began to advance economically, the challenge before India was to get recognition as a major power in South Asia and an important player in the global development. To achieve this objective, India had to recalculate its strategic options. India could no more depend on Soviet Union for military and diplomatic support. India was unsure, whether, the concessions it used to get during cold war in arms deal would be continued. It therefore, had to explore new suppliers including US. But it required that India should overcome its apprehensions and hesitations regarding developing relationship with US. The relationship with US also mattered more because of rise of China as a major economic power in early 1990s, which was bothering India. India realised that relationship with US would help India to serve its security interests which had come in trouble due to Soviet demise, thus fill in the vacuum. At the same time it would also serve the strategic interest of India—balancing power with China.

From US perspective, after the end of cold war and disintegration of Soviet Union, there was no need to look at India as Soviet friend. Further, India's policy of market reforms was considered as an open invitation for US. India gradually emerged the important trade partner of US resulting in increased Indo-US trade from $4.5 billion in 1988 to roughly $27 billion in 2005.[35] The leaders of both India and US showed their willingness to take steps to create an environment for India-US partnership. During the same period, US was concerned about rising economic power of

---

[35] Paul Kapur and Sumit Ganguly, "The transformation of India-US relations. An Explanation for the Rapprochement and Prospects for the Future," http://cisac.fsi.stanford.edu/sites/default/files/Kapur_Transformation_of_US_India_Relations.pdf accessed on 14 June 2016.

China as it was a direct threat to economic hegemony of US. For US, one of the major objective of its foreign policy was to contain influence of China. US visualized India as a balancer of China in its South Asia policy. In fact, rising Chinese power helped India and US to coincide their interests in Asia. Together, all these factors gradually, altered the nature of bilateral relationship between India and US in the period after cold war and the relationship between the two acquired significance on its own merits.

Dramatic geopolitical changes in the post-cold war period and the emerging global challenges, the shared national interests and common strategic objectives such as defeating terrorism, preventing weapons proliferation, and maintaining regional stability have created new possibilities for security cooperation between India and US. From Indian standpoint this relationship is important as it will enhance India's ability to bring and preserve the stability in the region, which is an important condition for her to emerge as a regional hegemon as well as global power. One major challenge is the relationship with Pakistan. While India's objective is to emerge a major power in Asia, Pakistan's objective is to prevent India's pre-dominance in the region. Another challenge is role of China in South Asia. China is expanding its influence in the region by way of investing in infrastructural facilities as well as in the areas of defence and security. During the cold war period, US had a very close defense relationship with Pakistan. US was the major supplier of defense equipment to Pakistan and also provided financial aid that strengthened Pakistan's position in the face of India. US tilt towards India and its support to India on political, economic, defense and international front will help calm down Pakistan in its relationship with India. Thus, whereas the strategic balance in South Asia is maintained by the nuclear balance of power, US plays an important role in maintaining strategic stability in the region.

The strategic partnership between India and US is an expression of power politics in the region. As close relationship of US with India results in tilting the balance of power between US and China, in favour of US, it also tilts the balance of power between India and Pakistan in favour of India. In this context the cooperation between India and US in the areas of counterterrorism, Defence and maritime security proves to be of immense significance. Since 2001, India and US are closely engaged in counter terrorism efforts which has become the main pillar of security relationship between India and US. Both share the common vision of security of South Asia—stability in Afghanistan and destroy terrorist networks targeting American and Indian people and interests. It has strengthened bilateral counterterrorism cooperation beyond Afghanistan since 2008. Apart from cooperation in anti-terrorism policy of US, US believes that as India's "military capabilities grow, [the country] will contribute to Asia as a net provider of security in the Indian Ocean and beyond."[36]

The current Indo-US rapprochement has been termed as 'irreversible' and is known as Strategic Partnership. Both states took several initiatives which lead them to develop a strong strategic partnership. This strategic partnership is comprised of a broader range of areas for mutual cooperation which includes economic, trade, space, nuclear technology, missile

---

[36] "US Gives India Policing Power in the Indian Ocean," Times of India (Delhi), February 3, 2013, accessed on 14 June 2016.

technology, and defense cooperation.[37] As US began to plan for withdrawal from Afghanistan, it is more interested in engaging in Asia economically. To achieve this objective, US has launched the idea of greater economic and infrastructural integration of the region for supporting political stability in the region. In 2011, US promoted "New Silk Road" strategy that would bring South Asia closer to Central Asia. Geographically, South and Central Asia historically served as interlinking trade routes. US believes that if this old trade route is revived it will help the integration of South Asia. It will help promote trade between Central Asia, South Asia and South East Asia as well as between the nations of South Asia. This connectivity between the nations of South Asia will help them realized their bilateral potential, attract the foreign direct investment, enhance energy security and boost people to people contacts. According to US, the economic potential of coherent and integrated South Asia is virtually unlimited and India which is the stronghold of South Asia and the most economically successful region can drive global politics and economics in future. US therefore is interested in building up strong economic and security partnership with India.

The Partnership Building

The first glimpse of cooperation was the 1985 Memorandum of understanding between India and US over the transfer of technology and the 1990 proposal introducing "a common strategic vision"[38] in 1995 during the visit of US

---

[37] Berkeley Journal of Social Sciences Vol. 1, No. 1, 1 Jan 2011 India-United States Strategic Partnership: Implications for Pakistan Syed Shahid Hussain Bukhari accessed on 3 August 2016.

[38] Berkeley Journal of Social Sciences Vol. 1, No. 1, 1 Jan 2011 India-United States Strategic Partnership: Implications for Pakistan Syed Shahid Hussain Bukhari, accessed on 3 August 2016.

Defense Secretary, William Perry to India agreement on defence cooperation was signed and the Joint India-United States steering committees were established to promote coordination between the armed and naval services of both countries.[39] During US President Clinton's visit to India in 2000 and later under President George Bush India and US took steps to institutionalize and intensify the mutual relationship. Democracy, economy and security were the three pillars of cooperation between India and US. In 2001 meeting between President Bush and Prime Minister Vajpayee agreed to expand their mutual relations in a variety of areas, which included economic, security, space, counterterrorism, arms sales, scientific collaboration, regional security, civilian nuclear safety, and joint military exercises. The Bush Administration was close to publicly recognizing India as a special partner, having concluded, like the Clinton Administration before it, that India must be the linchpin of US policy in South Asia despite American unhappiness about the Indian nuclear weapons program. Both administrations recognized that the post-Cold War upswing in bilateral relations needed to be accelerated, with trade playing an important role.[40] In December 2001, "the US-India Defense Policy Group met in New Delhi for the first time since India's 1998 nuclear tests and outlined a defense partnership based on regular and high-level policy dialogue.[41] Moreover, The

---

[39] Ibid.

[40] Polly Nayak US Security Policy in South Asia Since 9/11—Challenges and Implications for the Future Asia Pacific Centre for security studies February 2005 (http://apcss.org/Publications/Ocasional%20Papers/USSecurity3.pdf) accessed on 8 August 2016.

[41] K. Alan Kronstadt, India-US Relations, CRS Issue Brief for Congress Received through the CRS Web (http://fpc.state.gov/documents/organization/61525.pdf) accessed on 16 August 2016.

National Security Strategy 2002 of Bush Administration stated that "US interests require a strong relationship with India. We are the two largest democracies, committed to political freedom protected by representative government.[42] In the course of time, US-India strategic partnership started building up which included easing restrictions in the areas of dual-use high-technology goods, civil nuclear cooperation and civilian space cooperation and expanding dialogue on missile defense. This development was termed as 'Next Steps Strategic Partnership' (NSSP) which implied that US intended to help India to emerge a major power in the world.

US-India Nuclear Deal

The U.S.-India Nuclear Deal

Refer footnote 43

---

[42] Berkeley Journal of Social Sciences Vol. 1, No. 1, 1, Jan 2011 India-United States Strategic Partnership: Implications for Pakistan Syed Shahid Hussain Bukhari accessed on 3 August 2016.

[43] https://www.google.co.in/imgres, Indo-us-nuclear-deal accessed on 3 August 2016.

The nuclear deal between India and US in 2005 was a milestone in the India-US strategic partnership. This Civil Nuclear Deal brought a major transformation in India-US relations after 2005 as this deal generated an environment of trust for broadening the partnership between India and US. In the last ten years, the commercial engagement between India and US has grown significantly. US has become India's largest trading partner in goods and services as well as major supplier of arms. Further people to people contacts have increased and today more than 3 million people live in America and playing a major role in American economy and polity. Cooperation on counter-terrorism and intelligence sharing has expanded significantly and both are willing to avoid confrontation on the issues of global significance such as climate change. Today US views India as a potential great power in Asia and a balancer of China and it is willing to help India to increase India's comprehensive national power. One very important result of the nuclear deal is the removal of sanctions imposed on India by US after the 1974 nuclear tests. After US removed sanctions, India can import Uranium from multiple vendors and also can deal for purchase of new reactors that boosted the atomic power generation in India. The most significant is, US refusal to extend same kind of nuclear partnership with Pakistan and its refusal to mediate between India-Pakistan conflicts over Kashmir, thus upholding India's stand that Kashmir issue is a "bilateral" issue. This has further strengthened the trust relationship between India and US.

Source : http://swapsushias.blogspot.in/2011/08/us–indo–relations.html#.
WamTySgjE2w

MODI-OBAMA TALKS **The Outcome**	Civil Nuclear Agreement	Other issues
	Breakthrough in operationalisation of the deal stalled since 2005	● Bilateral Investment Treaty-to enhance the two-way commerce that has already touched a record USD 100 billion
	● **Indian liability law holds the suppliers directly liable in case of a nuclear accident** while countries like France and the US have asked India to follow global norms under which the primary liability lies with the operator	● Defence: India interested in 5 hi-tech military hardware items (out of 17 offered) of for co-production and co-development under DTTI.
	● Following the international norms will mean the government would have to pay the damages in case of an accident	● Terrorism: Bilateral security cooperation against terrorist groups, further enhancing counter-terrorism
	● US companies to assess the market and decide whether to partake in India's nuclear programme	● Regional cooperation: to advance peace, stability, prosperity in Asia Pacific and Indian Ocean
	● **Insurance liability clause**: India tells US that it will build a pool that will indemnify American reactor builders against liability in case of an accident	● Working on how to help in the transformation of Afghanistan
		● Social security agreement - for Indian professionals working in the US
	GRAPHICS	

Refer footnote 44

India and US: Joint Strategic Vision

India-US bilateral relations have developed into a "global strategic partnership", based on shared democratic values and increasing convergence of interests on bilateral, regional and global issues.[45] In 2005, India and US signed "New framework of India-US Defence relations". As a result, US-India defence trade, joint exercises, personnel exchanges, collaboration and cooperation in maritime security and counter-piracy, and exchanges have intensified and defence relationship has emerged as a new pillar of strategic relationship between India and US. The US and India strategic dialogue was initially initiated under President Bush. Pr. Obama renewed this dialogue in 2010. India was treated as indispensable partner. President Obama declared

---

[44] Barack Obama, Narendra Modi seal nuclear deal: 6 top points, http://www.financialexpress.com accessed on 3 August 2016.

[45] http://www.mea.gov.in/Portal/ForeignRelation/USA_Dec2014.pdf, accessed on 3 August 2016.

his firm belief that "the relationship between the United States and India will be a defining partnership in the 21st century."[46] President Obama visited India in November 2010. During his visit he gave a historic speech to a joint session of the Indian Parliament characterized the US-India partnership as serving three broad purposes:

(1) Promoting prosperity on both countries, especially through greater trade and two-way investment, and food security and health-related initiatives;

(2) Enhancing shared security by working together to prevent terrorist attacks, and;

(3) Strengthening democratic governance and human rights.[47]

Another Strategic Dialogue was held in New Delhi in July 2011. The resulting Joint Statement highlighted a bilateral commitment to "broaden and deepen the US-India global strategic partnership" in the cause of global stability and prosperity, and to enhance the partnership in numerous issue-areas. Among the notable clauses of the Statement were:

• a reaffirmation of the two countries' "commitment for consultation, coordination, and cooperation on Afghanistan," to include a reconciliation process there that is "Afghan-led, Afghan-owned, and inclusive";

---

[46] President Obama's June 3, 2010, remarks at http://www.whitehouse.gov/the-press-office/remarks-president-us-india-strategic-dialogue-reception, accessed on 3 August 2016.

[47] "Remarks by the President to the Joint Session of the Indian Parliament, New Delhi, India," White House release, November 8, 2010, accessed on 3 August 2015.

- a call for Pakistan "to move expeditiously in prosecuting those involved in the November 2008 Mumbai terrorist attack";

- a continued commitment to "full implementation of the US-India civil nuclear energy cooperation agreement"; and

- plans to resume technical-level negotiations on a bilateral investment treaty.[48]

India's Minister of External Affairs Shri S.M. Krishna and US Secretary of State Hillary Rodham Clinton met in Washington, DC, on June 13, 2012, for the third annual US-India Strategic Dialogue. The leaders reflected on the remarkable expansion and growth of the bilateral relationship since the inaugural Strategic Dialogue in 2010. They committed to further broaden and deepen the US-India global strategic partnership and charted a vision for the future, centred on promoting shared prosperity, peace and stability. Secretary Clinton and Minister Krishna affirmed the importance of maritime security, unimpeded commerce, and freedom of navigation, in accordance with international law, and the peaceful settlement of maritime disputes. The two sides agreed to continue to consult closely on key global issues, including bilateral exchanges and information sharing in areas such as counternarcotic, countering piracy, maritime safety, and humanitarian assistance/disaster relief. Determined to curb the problem of piracy off the coast of Somalia, both governments planned to improve coordination of their anti-piracy efforts. They also planned to cooperate in addressing the problem of hostage-taking by pirates. The

---

[48] India: Domestic Issues, Strategic Dynamics, and US Relations (https://www.fas.org/sgp/crs/row/RL33529.pdf) accessed on 6 August 2016.

same was reaffirmed in the "Strategic Dialogue" in 2013 and 2014.

During President Obama's visit to India in January 2015, US and India signed "US-India Joint Strategic Vision" for Asia-Pacific and Indian Ocean Region. This is considered as a major development in constructive Indo-US relations. The vision sets an agenda for Asia-Pacific and Indian Ocean region and outlines a more significant role for India in the region. India is expected to play a more active role in the security framework of region with special focus on maritime security. Maritime security is becoming increasingly important for India due to increasing presence of China in Indian Ocean region and South China Sea. India's "Look East Policy" has been transformed to the "Act East Policy"— laying the groundwork for an increased Indian presence in Southeast Asia.

Defence Cooperation

Since Independence of India, except the period between 1962-1965, India and US never had a serious security partnership. During India-China border war in 1962, US provided military assistance to India on India's request. US also gave military assistance to Pakistan, which Pakistan used against India in 1965 war. The security partnership between India and US ended in 1965 and the relationship between the two deteriorated. Improved US-China relationship in 1970s and continued relationship with Pakistan in 1980s, India began to think of Washington, Beijing and Islamabad as its own "axis of evil".[49]

---

[49] Stephen P. Cohen and Dhruva Jaishankar, "Indo-US Ties: The Ugly, the Bad and the Good" February 2009 http://www.brookings.edu/research/articles/2009/02/india-cohen accessed on 11 August 2015.

The defence relationship between India and US were renewed in the early 1990s. During first Gulf War India gave the US refuelling rights. Indo-US defence cooperation was strengthened by the Kicklighter proposals which recommended that Indo-US defence cooperation and military-to-military ties could be promoted through joint seminars, training, etc., and mooted the idea of expanding the defence cooperation framework. Executive Steering Groups were established in both the countries so as to deepen military-to-military cooperation. In February 1992, Indian and US Army and Air Force paratroopers held their first joint training exercise, codenamed 'Teak Iroquios', followed by another exercise in October 1993. Subsequently, the two nations' navies conducted joint exercises in the Indian Ocean in May 1992 and September 1995 and 1996, in keeping with the US policy of cooperative engagement with friendly militaries. In 1995, India and the US signed the Agreed Minutes of Defence Relations, which became the foundation of defence relations between New Delhi and Washington till the New Framework for the India-US Defence Relationship was signed in 2005. As per the 1995 agreement, bilateral cooperation was sought to be achieved through multi-interactions at the levels of: Defence Ministries, defence research and production as also at the level of senior officers from the Ministry of Defence and the US Office of the Secretary of Defense.[50] Thus the qualitative change began to occur in the relationship between India and

---

[50] Deba R. Mohanty & Uma Purushothaman, "India-US Defence Relations: In Search of a Direction" Observer Research Foundation, New Delhi, ORF Occasional Paper #23 August 2011 http://www.orfonline.org/cms/export/orfonline/modules/occasionalpaper/attachments/defence_1315307316072.pdf accessed on 3 August 2016.

US after the end cold war due to the international systemic changes and the changing perception of both towards each other.

There was a break in the relationship between the two after India conducted nuclear tests in 1998 and US imposed sanctions on India. Pr. Clinton partially lifted the sanctions and then Pr. Bush lifted the sanctions totally after 9/11 incident when India extended its whole heated support to US in its "war against terrorism". Lifting of sanctions led to the major improvement in the defence relationship between India and US. India and US began to consider each other as "natural ally".[51]

The first major arms sale to India was in 2002, when India bought 12 counter-battery radar sets ("Firefinder" radars) worth $190 million. In 2003, India became eligible for Excess Defense Articles (EDA) on grant basis under the US Foreign Assistance Act. This was meant to support the war on terrorism, promote interoperability of systems and to modernise previously sold equipment. This was followed by a momentous agreement, the Next Steps in Strategic Partnership (NSSP), which was signed in January 2004. The NSSP sought to expand cooperation on nuclear and civilian space technology, missile defence and dual use high technology trade. Another agreement on High Technology Trade resulted in the removal of ISRO from the US' Entity List. Later, after the tsunami struck in 2004, the armed forces of the two countries worked along with those of Japan and Australia in a multilateral disaster management

---

[51] C. Raja Mohan, Crossing the Rubicon: the shaping of India's New Foreign Policy, (Viking Penguin books, New Delhi, 2003).

effort, showing that cooperation in the military field was no longer constrained by bureaucratic formalities. The next big breakthrough came with the ten-year 'New Framework in the India-US Defence Relationship' signed on June 28, 2005, which charts a course for defence relations in the coming years as a key component of the burgeoning Indo-US strategic partnership. The Agreement aimed at advancing "shared security interests", namely:

- Maintaining security and stability;
- Defeating terrorism and violent religious extremism;
- Preventing the spread of weapons of mass destruction and associated materials, data, and technologies and;
- Protecting the free flow of commerce via land, air and sea lanes.

In pursuit of these interests, India and USA agreed to:

a) Conduct joint and combined exercises and exchanges;

b) Collaborate in multinational operations if it is in common interest;

c) Strengthen capabilities of militaries to promote security and defeat terrorism;

d) Promote regional and global peace and stability;

e) Enhance capabilities to combat the proliferation of weapons of mass destruction;

f) Increase opportunities for technology transfer, collaboration, coproduction, and research and development;

g) Expand collaboration relating to missile defence;

h) Strengthen abilities of the Armed Forces to respond quickly to disasters, including in combined operations;

i) Conduct successful peacekeeping operations;

j) Conduct and increase exchanges of intelligence.[52]

Since the signing of the New Framework for Defense Cooperation in 2005, the United States and India have made remarkable strides in their defense relations. India now holds more than 50 annual military exercises with the United States, more than any other country. Cumulative defense sales have grown from virtually zero to more than $8 billion. And high-level exchanges on defense issues also have increased. There have also been new opportunities for cooperation in homeland security that emerged in the wake of the 26/11 Mumbai terrorist attacks. The establishment last year of the US-India Homeland Security Dialogue was an important step to building cooperation in this key area. [53]

Fact Sheet: US-India Defense Relationship[54]

President Obama's visit resulted in several key defense outcomes, including finalizing the 2015 Framework for the US-India Defense Relationship. This Framework provides India and US with guiding principles for defense engagement for the coming decade, including military exchanges and exercises, a promising outlook on defense trade, and increasingly close consultations on regional security issues and maritime security.

---

[52] Deba R. Mohanty & Uma Purushothaman, "India-US Defence Relations: In Search of a Direction" Observer Reasearch Foundation, New Delhi, ORF Occasional Paper #23 August 2011 http://www.orfonline.org/cms/export/orfonline/modules/occasionalpaper/attachments/defence_1315307316072.pdf, accessed on 9 August 2015.

[53] S. Amer Latif and Nicholas Lombardo, "US-India Defense Trade opportunities for deepening the partnership" a report of the csis wadhwani chair in US-india policy studies (http://csis.org/files/publication/120703_Latif_USIndiaDefense_Web.pdf) accessed on 3 August 2016.

[54] http://archive.defense.gov/pubs/US-IND-Fact-Sheet.pdf accessed on 3 August 2016.

PARTNERSHIP
Defence equipment purchases from US

2005-2008 (total $3.25 billion)	
8 Boeing P-81 maritime aircraft	$2.1 bn
6 Super Hercules aircraft	$1 bn
20 GE F-404 engines for Tejas	$100 mn
USS Trenton	$50 mn
2009-2013 (total $5.74 billion)	
10 C-17 Globemaster III aircraft	$4.12 bn
6 additional Super Hercules aircraft	$1 bn
40 Harpoon anti-ship missiles	$370 mn
500 CBU-97 sensor-fused bombs	$250 mn
In the pipeline (total $8.35 billion)	
275 F-125 Honeywell engines for Jaguar	$2 bn
6 more C-17 Globemaster III aircraft	$2 bn
22 AH-64E Apache attack helicopters	$1.4 bn
4 additional Boeing P-81 maritime aircraft	$1 bn
15 Chinook CH-47F heavy lift helicopters	$1 bn
145 M777 guns from BAE Systems	$700 mn
50 General Electric F-404 engines for Tejas	$250 mn

Refer footnote 55

US-India Defense Relationship: Recent Milestones

*   2005—The United States and India sign the New
    Framework for the India-US Defense Relationship,
    ushering in a decade of tremendous growth in the defense
    relationship and setting the US and India on a path to
    increasingly broad, complex and strategic cooperation.

*   2012—Secretary Panetta appoints then Deputy Secretary
    of Defense Carter to lead a bold, new initiative now known

---

[55] Ajai Shukla, "India-US defence ties grow with assertive Modi Govt"
http://www.business-standard.com/article/economy-policy/india-us-
defence-ties-grow-with-assertive-modi-govt-115012100021_1.html, Jan,
21, 2015 accessed on 3 August 2016.

as the Defense Technology and Trade Initiative (DTTI). DTTI, launched in 2012, is an unprecedented joint endeavour that brings sustained leadership focus to the bilateral defense trade relationship, creates opportunities for US-India co-production and co-development, and fosters more sophisticated science and technology cooperation, all while ensuring that bureaucratic processes and procedures do not stand in the way of the progress.

• 2014—President Obama and former Prime Minister Singh endorse the India-US Declaration on Defense Cooperation, a document that reflects the United States' and India's commitment to a long-term strategic partnership, through which our countries cooperate to increase the security and prosperity of our citizens and the global community.

India-U.S. Defense Exercises

The American & Indian militaries have participated in a number of bilateral exercises, including YUDH ABHYAS, COPE INDIA, MALABAR & VAJRA PRAHAR.	In 2014, India took part for the first time in the multilateral maritime exercise RIMPAC. It has also participated in RED FLAG.
India conducts more military exercises with the U.S. than with any other country. The U.S. Army, Air Force, Marines, Navy & Special Forces have participated in excercises with India.	Australia, Japan & Singapore have also participated in MALABAR. Japan took part in 2014. Recently, the Indian PM endorsed Japan's continued participation.

Source: U.S. Department of Defense; The White House; Embassy of India, Washington, D.C.   Tanvi Madan, The Brookings Institution

Refer footnote 56

---

[56] http://www.brookings.edu/blogs/up-front/posts/2014/09/26/us-india-relations-in-14-charts-madan accessed on 12 August 2016.

Analysing the US-India Defence Partnership

Defence partnership between India and US is considered as brightest spot in the India-US relationship. The Asia-Pacific policy of India and US is congruent—both aim at preserving regional stability in Asia-Pacific and preventing use of force to resolve territorial and maritime disputes and preventing China's territorial assertions.

The defence agreement will act as a foundation to enhance the defence trade and commerce between India and US. However, the defence relations between the two are not free from challenges.

The defence objectives of India and US are clearly different from each other. US is interested in defence trade with India, as US sees India as a prominent market and US economy would prosper on due to the weapons trade. But this is not the sole purpose. US aims to play a major role in the politics of Asia by involving intensely in the security engagements in Asia. To attain this objective US sees India as a major defence partner. India on the other hand in interested in engaging with US for the purpose of much needed technology transfer which is required for modernization of its defence capabilities. India thus expects US help and cooperation in the production of defence equipment as well as in building indigenous defence capabilities. However there may be a discrepancy between what kind of defence technology US shares with India and what type of technology India is expecting from US. If divergence between what US provides and what India expects is beyond the acceptable limits it would a major obstacle in the future development of healthy defence relationship between the two.

India, however, is apprehensive about the achievement of this objective on the ground that as US is engaged in arms sales to India, it also sales arms to Pakistan. Thus, if Pakistan is getting same help from US as India gets, it will lead to increasing deterrence in South Asia and more strained relationship between India and Pakistan. The strains can be developed over this issue between India and US at any point which can have a significant impact on the defence trade between the two in future. To avoid such problems in the relationship between the two, the role of bureaucracy in both the nations is equally important. It should work to develop trust, help to resolve issues and ensure transparency of the relationship and thus pave the way for more seamless collaboration. Even the involvement of civil society is important in this process as it helps avoid misperceptions about other's motives, attitudes and policies.

Maritime Security and Interests

India-US engagement has acquired a new dimension with the adoption of "US-India Joint Strategic Vision for the Asia-Pacific and Indian Ocean Region" that outlines a new role for both India and US in protections of their regional security interests. This policy seeks to increase maritime cooperation between the two countries. The declaration affirms the shared vision for promising prosperity and stability in the region, besides assuring concrete understandings and partnerships in the area of defence relations.[57] In the official release of the Bureau of South and Central Asian Affairs, US, it is stated

---

[57] Vivek Mishra, India-US joint strategic vision: Implications for the Indo-Pacific (http://www.indiawrites.org/diplomacy/india-us-joint-strategic-vision-implications-for-the-indo-pacific/) accessed on 7 September 2016.

that "For the first time in our bilateral relations, there can be no doubt about the strength of our joint strategic vision. Our two countries are indispensable partners in promoting peace, prosperity, and stability in the Indo-Pacific region. We are drivers of growth across the region and around the world. And we are net providers of security, together ensuring freedom of navigation and safeguarding maritime security. These values are clearly reflected in our Joint Strategic Vision for the Asia-Pacific and Indian Ocean Region, leaving no doubt about our commitment to a peaceful, prosperous, and stable Asia in the 21st century. As the President said during his visit, the progress we have made across every aspect of the relationship demonstrates that the United States and India are not just natural partners—but that America can be India's best partner."[58]

India's Stakes in Asia-Pacific and Indian Ocean Region

India always desired to play a prominent role as security provider in Asia-Pacific but was aware that, China's power ambitions will never allow India to play such a role. The relationship with US therefore becomes all the more significant for India. As both India and US consider China's assertive policies as threat to the security complex of the region, together both of them can restrict China and play more active role in the emerging security architecture of Indo-Pacific.

In the early 1990s, India adopted 'Look East' policy in order to engage economically with the prosperous nations of South

---

[58] Nisha Desai Biswal, "The United States and India: A Future of Friendship" http://www.state.gov/p/sca/rls/rmks/2015/237274.htm, accessed on 11 october 2016.

East Asia. India's increasing engagement with South East Asia is getting challenged by the disputes in South China Sea. The dispute involves both the territorial and maritime claims of various sovereign states within the region such as Brunei, Indonesia, Malaysia, Philippines, Vietnam, Taiwan and China. The disputes revolve around several issues such as maritime boundaries, overlapping of Exclusive Economic zones, acquiring fishing area, exploitation of crude oil and natural gas as well as the strategic control of important shipping lanes. As China is one party in most of these disputes, an agreement was reached. A serious attempt was made to resolve the disputes by establishing preliminary guidelines. Shortly after China and Vietnam signed an agreement for the resolution of dispute in South China Sea, ONGC-India declared that its overseas arm, ONGC Videsh limited had signed three year agreement with Petro Vietnam for developing long-term co-operation in the oil sector and one part of the agreement allows India to explore in specified blocs of South China Sea. China claims that the areas where India intends to conduct exploration activities come under Chinese jurisdiction. The non-recognition of India's claims by China is a major problem area in developing strategic and economic relationship between India and ASEAN.

China has been acquiring naval facilities along the crucial choke-points in the Indian Ocean not only to serve its economic interests but also to enhance its strategic presence in the region. China realizes that its maritime strength will give it the strategic leverage it needs to emerge as the regional hegemon and a potential superpower. China's growing dependence on maritime space and resources is reflected in the Chinese aspiration to expand its influence and to ultimately dominate the strategic environment of the Indian Ocean region. China's increasing reliance on bases across the Indian Ocean region is a response to its perceived vulnerability, given the logistical constraints that it faces due to the distance of the Indian Ocean waters from its own territory. Yet, China is consolidating power over the South China Sea and the Indian Ocean with an eye on India.[59] This strategy is called "string of pearls" and has considerably increased China's strategic depth. Thus increasing Chinese presence in the Indian Ocean region is a direct threat to India's sphere of strategic influence.

US Interest in South China Sea and Indian Ocean

The South China Sea is an important trade route for intra-regional and international trade. More than 5 Trillion dollars' worth of trade passes through these waters each year including more than 1 trillion with US. US therefore is interested in unhindered access to South China Sea. Also unhindered access sustains US ability to project military power not just in East Asia, but around the world as, many naval vessels from the West Coast and Japan pass through the South China Sea to Indian Ocean and Persian Gulf.[60] The US interests in South China Sea are threatened by China. China interprets the rights of coastal States falling in the Exclusive Economic Zones that suits its own security interests. It tries to limit the military activities in this zone including US surveillance

---

[59] Harsh V. Pant, "China's Naval Expansion in the Indian Ocean and India-China Rivalry" The Asia Pacific Journal – Japan focus http://japanfocus.org/-harsh_v_-pant/3353/article.html accessed on 3 August 2016.

[60] Michael A. McDevitt • M. Taylor Fravel • Lewis M. Stern, "The Long Littoral Project: South China Sea A Maritime Perspective on Indo-Pacific Security"(https://www.cna.org/CNA_files/PDF/IRP-2012-U-2321-Final.pdf) accessed on 3 August 2016.

and exploration, close to China's coast. The fear is that China may impose similar restrictions in the entire South China Sea. To sustain its claims over South China Sea, China is engaged in modernizing its navy which creates security threats for other coastal States. The possibility of frequent use of coercive measures, the possibility of armed conflicts and the consequent increased investments of coastal State in the modernization of navy undermines the peace and stability in the region. Such situations creates dilemma for United States as it has to maintain its commitments to allies in the region, at the same time continue with the cooperative relationship with China. In July 2010, in the annual meeting of ASEAN Regional Forum, US Secretary of State Hillary Clinton made a public statement regarding US policy of opposition to "the use or threat of force by any claimant" and "not taking sides" in competing territorial claims. Though China was not clearly mentioned, the US statement clearly directed against China.[61] As US seems to be taking sides of the nations of South East Asia, China might see US as a growing threat on the other hand, if ASEAN nations see US supporting them, they may drag US into conflicts in South China Sea. China fears that India-US maritime cooperation aims at building anti-China coalition in the Indo-Pacific region.

The Malabar naval exercise was started initially as a bilateral naval drill between the Indian and the United States navies. Japan became a permanent member of the Malabar exercise in 2015.

(https://swarajyamag.com/defence/malabar-naval-exercise-a-show-of-strength-in-the-bay-of-bengal)

---

[61]Michael A. McDevitt • M. Taylor Fravel • Lewis M. Stern, "The Long Littoral Project: South China Sea A Maritime Perspective on Indo-Pacific Security"(https://www.cna.org/CNA_files/PDF/IRP-2012-U-2321-Final.pdf) accessed on 5 September 2016.

STARING DRAGON **IN THE EYE?**

US, India concerned about Chinese muscle-flexing in Indian Ocean

➤ Plan to **deepen Malabar series** by adding army and air force components to naval exercise	➤ More exercises around **nuclear submarines and aircraft carrier** likely
➤ More **countries may be invited** to Malabar series making it a trilateral exercise	➤ **Chinese moves** in South China Sea **found mention in joint statement** during the PM's US visit

Refer footnote 62

The 19th India-US Joint Naval exercise "Malabar" in the Bay of Bengal was held in October 2015. Presence of Japan Navy in this exercise made it a trilateral exercise aimed at countering growing Chinese presence in the Indian Ocean Region.[63] US navy is conducting maritime patrols within the 12-mile territorial zone around China's recently reclaimed islands in the disputed Spratly archipelago, maritime tensions in the Pacific are at an all-time high. In response to Washington's rebalance to Asia, Beijing has hardened its maritime posture in the Western Pacific. From an Indian perspective, the United States' endorsement of "freedom of navigation" patrols in the South China Sea might leave China with little option but to expand its military maritime

---

[62] Josy Joseph, "Eye on China, India and US set to ramp up joint naval drills" http://timesofindia.indiatimes.com/india/Eye-on-China-India-and-US-set-to-ramp-up-joint-naval-drills/articleshow/45075908.cms, Nov 8, 2014, accessed on 5 September 2016.

[63] Abhijit Singh, "Malabar 2015: Strategic Power Py in the Indian Ocean" http://thediplomat.com/2015/10/malabar-2015-strategic-power-play-in-the-indian-ocean/ accessed on 5 September 2016.

presence in the wider Indo-Pacific—if only to show the US and its allies that Chinese maritime power cannot be contained within China's near-seas.[64]

US-India: Convergences in the Indo-Pacific

After US withdrawal from Afghanistan, US aims to engage in Asia economically and also wishes to play a meaningful role in regional integration and engagements in Indo-Pacific. US believes that India can cooperate with US in achieving this objective due to the common interests of India and US. In the post-cold war period India adopted "Look East" policy for achieving its objective of economic growth. This policy now has been transformed into "Act East" policy. Bridging the gap between South and South East Asia through Indo-Pacific is the part of this policy. India is taking initiative in developing infrastructure, construction of highways and promotion of trade connectivity. US is interested in building up relationship with Bangladesh and Myanmar, the nations connected with India, that would facilitate energy trade and maritime linkage with US and for the purpose wants to promote Indo-Pacific Economic Corridor that would connect South Asia, South East Asia and Central Asia. Thus India's interest in Eastward expansion and US interest in Indo-Pacific move on the same track and thus are complementary which proves to be a strong ground for India-US cooperation. However, China with a dominant presence and role in the Asia-Pacific, a desire to increase its presence in the Indian Ocean and an already well-connected (mainly through energy pipelines) presence in Central Asia makes for a formidable impediment in the way of realisation

---

[64] ibid.

of the joint strategic vision by India and the US in both the Asia-Pacific and the Indo-Pacific.[65]

Global Commons

Another area of concern regarding the cooperation between India and US in the area of control over global commons. The "Global Commons" refers to resource domains or areas that lie outside of the political reach of any one nation State. International law identifies four global commons namely: the High Seas; the Atmosphere; Antarctica; and, Outer Space. These areas have historically been guided by the principle of the common heritage of humankind— the open access doctrine or themare liberum (free sea for everyone) in the case of the High Seas.[66] In other words, these are the resources owned by everyone. They are the resources accessible to all but owned by none. As defined by US Department of Defence the global commons comprise the geographic and virtual realms of "space, international waters and airspace, and cyberspace".[67] The commons are seen as the essential channels of US national power in a rapidly globalizing and increasingly interconnected world. There exists a close relationship between maritime power and the ability to maintain the sea lines of communications with economic expansion and the impact on overall national

---

[65] Vivek Mishra, India-US joint strategic vision: Implications for the Indo-Pacific (http://www.indiawrites.org/diplomacy/india-us-joint-strategic-vision-implications-for-the-indo-pacific/) accessed on 5 September 2016.

[66] http://www.unep.org/delc/GlobalCommons/tabid/54404/ accessed on 9 September 2016.

[67] Mark E. Redden and Michael P. Hughes, Global Commons and Domain Interrelationships: Time for a New Conceptual Framework? Strategic Forum November 2010 accessed on 11 September 2016.

power. Attainment of US strategic, economic, informational, and military objectives is contingent upon assured access to, and freedom of action within, the commons. Accordingly, global commons access must remain at the forefront of US national security imperatives.[68]

US always had a hegemonic control over those power domains. But in the last decade the US hegemony has been challenged by rising powers and the diffusion of technological capabilities. Current security concerns of US include the challenge of managing control over commons in the multipolar world, reframing the international rules for managing global commons and also to decide who will be the potential partner of US in this venture.

There is unprecedented increase in China's strategic and military capacity in the last decade. US therefore, looks at China as a major competitor. US has two options—either to accommodate China in its security structure to manage global commons or to consider India as a potential partner to check and balance China. However, India-US Joint Strategic Vision does not mention India's role as a partner in managing global commons. In fact in this sphere, US equates India with China and Russia that challenge hitherto uncontested role of US in managing global common. As Pentagon strategists Michele Flournoy and Shawn Brimley argue, "rising powers will not simply be content to simply acquiesce to America's role as uncontested guarantor of the global commons. Countries such as China, India, and Russia will demand a role in maintaining the international system

---

[68] Redden, Mark E.; Hughes, Michael P., Defense Planning Paradigms and the Global Commons Joint Force Quarterly accessed on 11 September 2016.

in ways commensurate with their perceived power and national interests.[69]

Current US-India cooperation for Maritime security has however raised expectations that there are further possibilities of cooperation between India and US over managing other global commons. There seems to have common understanding between them, of the importance of adherence to International Law and generally avoiding any large scale misadventures by both of them. Further growing cooperation of India and US in Information Technology sector, development of space technology and international space law require that both of them also cooperate in constructing a framework of rules regarding cyber space, space, international waters and airspace. As a growing power, India's global interests match with the other major power's interests especially with US in the matters of global common and therefore, India can help in devising a regime for global commons. As a result, India and US are expected to work together in building norms and institutions for the maintenance of global commons.

Conclusion

India and US relationship that began as a relationship of arms trade and economic exchanges in the other areas has now transformed into strategic partnership. India is facing rising security threats due to continued low intensity conflicts with Pakistan, Chinese incursions into Indian Territory, and the new threats from ISIS. In such situations, India has to strengthen its military power and relationship with US will

---

[69] C. Raja Mohan, "Rising India: Partner in Shaping the Global Commons?" http://csis.org/files/publication/twq10julymohan.pdf accessed on 5 September 2016.

help India to reinforce its military might. Further US and India have several common interests that include containing China's growing influence, Russia's growing defence relationship with Pakistan and the possibility of Russia-China-Pakistan axis, post US withdrawal restructuring of Afghanistan, maritime security in Asia and dealing with the terrorist threats. The deeper defence relationship between the two is mutually advantageous in the long run.

There are however several problem areas. America's defence relationship with Pakistan and India's relations with Russia for transfer of sensitive technology is a hitch in India-US relationship. Currently India-US defence relationship is a buyer-seller relationship. India does not have a strong defence manufacturing sector. India therefore depends to a great extent on foreign powers for its defence needs. India is expecting that this buyer-seller relationship between India and US should turn into a partnership for development and production of defence equipment. This is the crux of present India-US defence agreement.

CHAPTER 4

US Initiatives in India

India is the second most populous country in the world and has undergone tremendous transition since the economic reforms of 1991. Even in the uncertain global economic conditions, India has maintained around 6% annual economic growth and has registered itself as a significant global economic player. Consistent growth in the domestic demand in India and the policy decision of opening many sectors to Foreign Direct Investment have created opportunities for many outside industries to invest in India. Further India is also known for its highly skilled labour force, well versed with English language and western culture. Hence the companies are interested in transferring some of the activities in India and set up the Research and Development facilities in India where the young, talented and highly educated Indian professional can be accommodated. As India has invited the FDI, even Indian companies have become active at the global level, through acquisition of foreign companies and establishing the business operations beyond India, thus emerging as the world economic actor.

India's large population, large size, largest free market economy and status of a giant in South Asia makes it the most important partner of US—the partnership which is mutually beneficial. To advance Indian prosperity and perpetuate American prosperity, the first order of business is for the two private sectors to do more together.[70] The relationship between India and US revolves around business opportunities and economic gains. Therefore both are interested in the economic growth of each other and the collaborative efforts for economic growth.

Improved bilateral ties between India and US is a check over the growing authoritarianism in China and Russia. Clear shift to multipolar world leading to rise of new powers and their assertive policies are lessening US abilities to achieve its international goals. Weakening US economy is another constraint factor. Further, Asia's gradual emergence as economic powerhouse, and increasing geopolitical influence of Asia tend to change the global balance of power challenging US pre-eminence in the long term. Again the centre of principle international threats such as terrorism, nuclear proliferation are centred in and around Asia and it is a major challenge for US to deal with these threats. Lasting economic constrains along with the rising and competing power centres require US to rebuild closer relations with Asia, especially India. US has a vision for democratic world and working together with Asia's largest democracy will create the environment for democratic world. During the sluggish economic phase of US, India is exhibiting a trend towards sustained economic growth. India's economic growth results in increasing consumption. This consumption led growth results in rise in global demand. India's need

---

[70] Laveesh Bhandari, Jeremy Carl, Bibek Debroy, Michelle Kaffenberger, Pravakar Sahoo and Derek Scissors, Ph.D., "Unleashing the Market in the India-US Economic Relationship, Part 1" Special Report #124 on Asia and the Pacific, January 7, 2013, http://www.heritage.org/research/reports/2013/01/unleashing-the-market-in-the-india-us-economic-relationship-part-1 accessed on 5 September 2016.

for trade and FDI is an opportunity for US companies and investors ensuring sustained and potentially high returns. Due to China's inward looking policy of favouring domestic investments, India becomes more attractive for US. Thus as India grows economically it will help the economic recovery of US. Ample high-skilled workforce and technological advancement in India can prove advantageous for US firms for their research and innovation.

According to the Task Force recommendations, after the successful collaborations between India and US in the areas of defence and strategic cooperation in the last decade, the US aims at developing closer economic ties with India. Collaborating with India in trade and other areas of economic engagement is now at the top of the US-India bilateral agenda. The task force report calls for transforming economic relations in the way defense and strategic cooperation was recast over the past decade.

While the United States and India have substantial shared interests in several global issues, the Task Force identifies four specific areas for joint ventures: the cyber domain, global health, climate change and clean energy, and democracy.[71] India has the technical capabilities as well as talent and therefore it is possible for India and US to work together in these areas. India-America partnership is desirable in the areas of climate change, clean energy and promotion of democracy. It is widely held that India and US will be successful associates as has been demonstrated in the areas such as IT and medical field.

---

[71] Working with rising India—A joint venture for the new century—Task Force Report, http://www.cfr.org/india/working-rising-india/p37233 accessed on 12 September 2016.

The American companies in India started investing in India in the later half of 1990s. This was a period when Indian economy had already started growing in various sectors like Technology, Colas, Agriculture, Automobiles, Equipment, Finance and Banking. The companies gained huge profits. According to the American Chamber of Commerce in India, their membership base has soared up from zero in 1992 to more than 300. However, the major success in terms of investment and growth came in technology sector. Many of the top IT companies in India are American. In fact, out of the top 20 IT companies operating in India, 9 are from the US. These American companies in India account for about 37% of the turnover of the top 20 firms operating in India. However the growth of the American companies in India is not limited to IT or manufacturing only. India has a vast market of agriculture, which employs almost 70% of the population either directly or indirectly.[72] The largest recipient of US FDI in the last decade has been the services sector, manufacturing sector, Pharmaceuticals, IT, consulting and automobiles. The American engagement with India has produced several positive results. American firms in India have helped generating employment. They employ Indian scientists, and engineers. The other important benefits are the access to improved technology, skill upgradation, raising the level of research and development, increasing productivity of domestic firms, etc. These benefits are contributing to economic growth of India to a great extent.

US engagement with India grew substantially since 2000, though from a small base. The value of US exports of goods

---

[72] "American Companies in India" http://business.mapsofindia.com/india-company/america.html accessed on 5 September 2016.

and services to India in 2013 was 5.5 times larger than in 2000, US FDI in India was 10.2 times larger, and sales by affiliates of US companies in India were 13.5 times larger.

The United States is an important source of goods, services, and capital in the Indian market. It is India's fifth-largest source of FDI, following Mauritius, Singapore, the United Kingdom, and Japan. It is the fifth-largest exporter of goods to the Indian market, following China, the United Arab Emirates, Saudi Arabia and Switzerland. Between 2000 and 2013, US exports of goods to India grew at an average annual rate of 15.8 percent and US exports of services grew at an average annual rate of 13.2 percent. Growth slowed significantly after 2007, when the average annual growth rate of US exports of services dropped to 7.8 percent and the average annual growth rate of US exports of goods dropped to 7.1 percent. US education services exports have also expanded in recent years. Increasing numbers of Indians have been going overseas to study and nearly 100,000 Indian students are currently studying in the United States. US education exports to India have grown at an 8.4 percent annual rate since 2006.[73]

Why US is Interested in Investing in India

Indian economy is the fast growing economy with the rate of 7-8% and the growth rate is likely to remain constant whereas US economy grows at around 3% per annum. With this growth rate, India is expected to be the 3rd largest economy by

---

[73] "Trade, Investment, and Industrial Policies in India: Effects on the US Economy" United States International Trade Commission report December 2014 Publication Number: 4501 Investigation Number: 332-543 https://www.usitc.gov/publications/332/pub4,501_2.pdf accessed on 10 September 2016.

2030 after US and China. The economic reforms adopted by the Government of India and relaxation in FDI have created positive business environment and ease of doing business. This has made investing in India's growth an opportunity for US. In the last two decades American companies' investment in India has grown substantially. Expertise and technologies offered by American companies will significantly contribute to social development initiatives like public distribution systems, financial inclusion, healthcare & education and thus would provide solutions for India's vision of Digital India, Make in India, Smart Cities, and Skill India, etc.

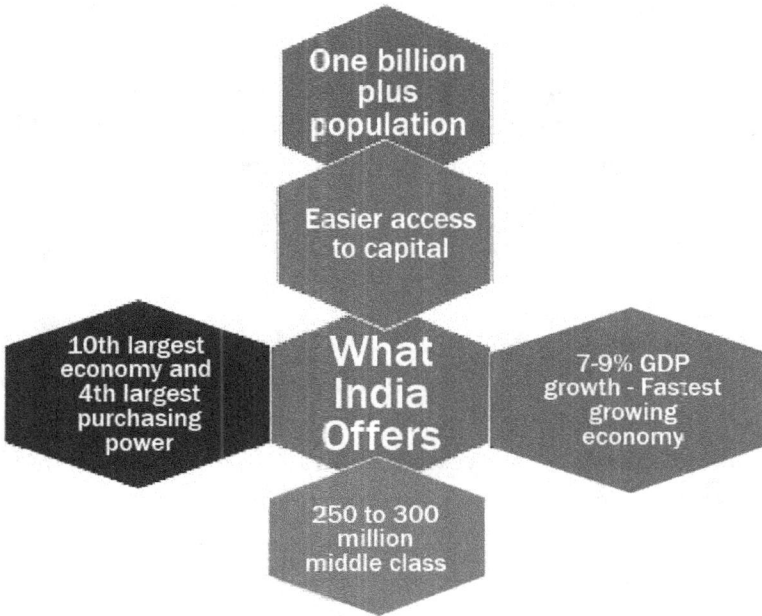

The BJP's 2014 election manifesto promised to increase economic growth and job creation through "consistent, long-term" policies. These policies included opening up certain sectors to foreign direct investment (FDI), providing predictable taxation policies, simplifying doing business, encouraging manufacturing in India, and improving infrastructure.[74] The Modi government has introduced several economic initiatives to restructure India's economy, all of which seek to impact India's trade and investment policies. These initiatives link long-term economic goals with near-term changes to policies and practices, and will sometimes rely on the participation and cooperation of foreign companies to succeed.[75] Modi's focus on business and his pragmatism provide the United States an opportunity for a fresh look at its relationship with India. Once inextricably engaged, America will find India a more reliable and trusting partner for long times to come.[76] In US policy of broadening its global spectrum and influence, a far reaching and close partnership with India occupies a prominent place as the interests and the values of India match and complement US strategy. India's size, geographical location, stable democracy and market led economic growth make it an essential player in the new global order. Building India-US partnership thus becomes a need for an hour.

The commercial relationship between India and US has been elevated in the second term of Pr. Barack Obama, especially after BJP Government led by Narendra Modi Government comes to power. US investments in India have been stepped up and it outpaces US investment in China.[77]

---

[74] BJP, Election Manifesto 2014, April 7, 2014, 26–30. accessed on 5 November 2016.

[75] Trade and Investment Policies in India, 2014–2015, https://www.usitc.gov/publications/332/pub4566.pdf

[76] Vinod Dham, "What the United States can gain from working closer with India" September 29, 2014, https://www.washingtonpost.com/news/innovations/wp/2014/09/29/what-the-united-states-can-gain-from-working-closer-with-india/ accessed on 5 September 2016.

[77] Dipanjan Roy, Economic Times, 31st March 2016.

The highlights of this investment are as follows[78]:

1. 30 US companies have invested $15 billion in last 1 and half year

2. 50 US firms are expected to ink over $27 billion deals over next year

3. American FDI in India estimated at $28 billion in 2014

4. Cumulative FDI inflows from the US from April 2000 to September 2014 were $13.19 billion

5. This was nearly 6% of total FDI into India, making US the 6th largest source of FDI.

The important areas covered by US investment initiative include FDI, Portfolio investment, Capital Market development and financing of infrastructure and US-India Infrastructure Collaboration Platform which would facilitate use of US technology to meet India's infrastructure needs. This statistics shows that US is emerging as India's largest trade and investment partner and is engaged with India at various levels of economic cooperation.

According to the report published by Academic Foundation, New Delhi in 2014, "Impact of American Investment in India" by Saon Ray, Smita Miglani and Neha Malik, US has emerged India's largest trade and investment partner and is engaged at various levels of economic cooperation.

The largest recipient of US FDI in the last few years has been the services sector, followed by manufacturing. Sectors with the largest US FDI inflows during 2004-12 were financial services, food and beverages and construction.

---

[78] US India Business Council, US bureau of Economic Analysis accessed on 5 September 2016.

India-U.S. Trade and Investment

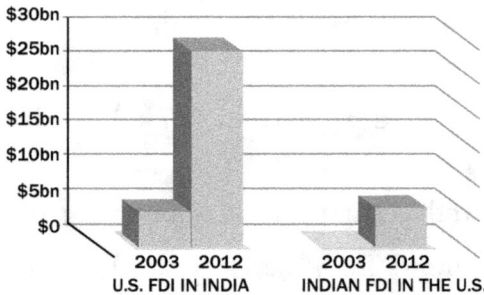

In terms of total trade, the U.S. is India's largest trading partner ...but there's immense room for growth. China-U.S. trade, for example, is over 5 times more than India-U.S. trade.

India is the 8th fastest growing source of foreign direct investment in the U.S.

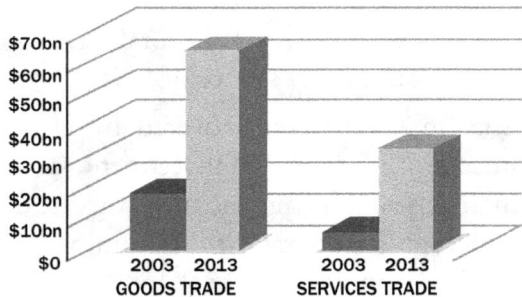

Refer footnote 79

The total overall impact of US FDI is high in the Service sector, followed by manufacturing, finance, Fast Moving Consumer Goods, IT, Pharmaceuticals, consulting and automobiles. India benefits from the direct inflow of capital that results in:

1. Employment generation and skill development
2. Linkages and spillover to domestic firms and increasing productivity of domestic firms,
3. Technology difusion and knowledge transfer
4. Raising the level of Research and development

---

[79] http://www.brookings.edu/blogs/up-front/posts/2014/09/26-us-india-relations-in-14-charts-madan, accessed on 5 September 2016.

5. Trade

6. Best practices

7. Economic growth.

The below graph shows the rising US foreign direct investment in India. 2005 onwards there is a consistent growth in the foreign direct investment. And after BJP Government came to power in 2014, the US FDI has increased considerably.

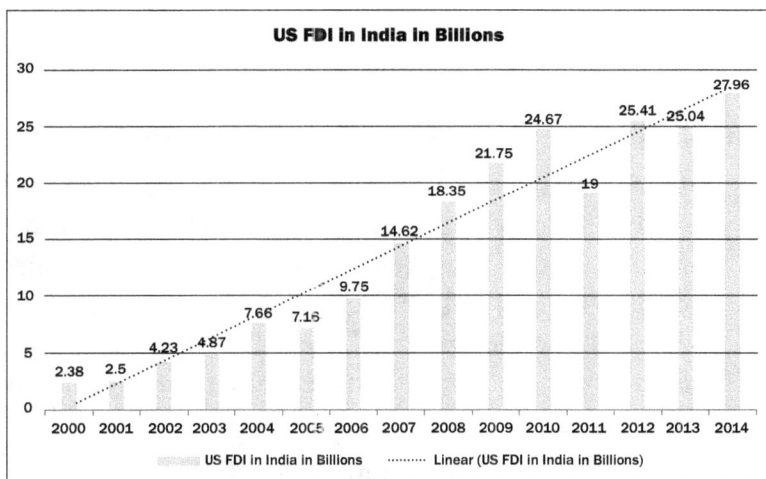

US FDI in India in Billions

Refer footnote 80

The prominent reasons for the increased FDI is the changes in India's foreign economic policy.

1. The Policy of allowing full foreign ownership in agriculture sector, specifically in the development and production of seeds and planting material, animal husbandry, aquaculture under controlled conditions, services related to agribusiness and related sectors.

---

[80] http://www.statista.com/statistics/188633/united-states-direct-investments-in-india-since-2000/ accessed on 11 September 2016.

2. Removal of cap of 51% on foreign investment, allowing 100% investment in single brand retail.

3. Merger/demerger of Indian company from foreign company and vice versa is allowed.

4. The concept of CSR—Corporate Social Responsibility. Every company having a net worth of ₹5 billion or more, or a turnover of ₹10 billion or more or a net profit of ₹50 million or more during any financial year shall ensure that in every financial year, it shall spent at least 2% of its average net profit for Corporate Social Responsibility.

Impact of American FDI on Selected Sectors

1. Automobile and Auto Components sector—The US based Ford India Private Limited and General Motors India Private Limited have vehicle manufacturing facilities and engine plats in India. General Motors in involved in engineering, design and Research and Development activities for developing alternative environment friendly technologies of future.

   Delphi India was incorporated in 1995 as a wholly owned subsidiary of Delphi and specializes in the design and production of a wide range of automotive products and electronics.

2. The financial and banking sector—American banks are usually wholly owned subsidiaries of the parent company as prescribed by Reserve Bank of India. Some American banks have set up Non-Banking Financial Company entity such as wealth and/or asset management business and investment advisory services.

3. Fast moving consumer goods—It is the fourth largest sector in Indian economy and expected to grow to USD

74 billion by 2018. 100% foreign equity is allowed in single retail brand and up to 51% is allowed in multi-brand retail. American companies such as Proctor and Gamble, PepsiCo Inc., Coca-Cola, and Amway sell consumer products directly in India.

4. The Pharmaceutical sector—Indian Pharmaceutical industry is the 3rd largest in the world in terms of volume. There is considerable inflow of US investment such as Pfizer Inc., Merck Inc., Mylan Inc. and Abbott Lab. US companies have partnered with Indian companies and also have entered into alliances with local generic pharmaceutical companies to jointly manufacture and market drugs. They are also active in over-the-counter drug market (drug sold without prescription) and India serves as the manufacturing location for OTC products. In alliance with Indian companies they are involved in marketing drugs in offshore markets, development and manufacturing of vaccines and other bio pharmaceutical products, develop, manufacture, supply and commercialise high value generic biologic compound for global markets, conducting clinical trials and research.

5. Consulting—Consulting is categorised into management consultancy and engineering consultancy. US companies are involved in management consultancy that comprise companies involved in accountancy, and other professional services such as audit, assurance, tax and advisory. Research, communication skills, HR management, Knowledge transmission are the important concerns of such companies. The American companies involved in management consultancy have taken initiative for organizing programmes for skill upgradation, leadership training programmes and such others.

Impact of American FDI on Selected Sectors

Sl. No.	Sector	Areas of Operations	Contribution
1	Automobile and Auto components • Ford India, General Motors, Delphi India	• Manufacturing: Passenger cars; engines and critical components • Back-end operations: IT, accounting and finance, financial services and automotive operations support, global analytics and engineering services.	• Brought in latest technologies • Manufacturing for export markets
2	Banking and Finance • American Express Banking Corporation, Bank of America, Citibank N.A. and J.P. Morgan Chase Bank N.A, The Bank of New York Mellon Corporation and Wells Fargo Bank	• Asset management business, investment advisory services • Data management • Credit research	• Generation of employment • Network of online banking • Promotion of plastic money
3	Information Technology • Microsoft, Oracle, Intel	• Software products, engineering • Research and Development • Training, system integration • Consultation, data modelling • BPOs	• Generation of employment • Improvement in HR skills • Increase in competitiveness • Bring in capital and technology
4	Fast Moving Consumer Goods • Proctor and Gamble, PepsiCo Inc, Coca-Cola, Amway	• foods, cleaning agents and personal care products • skin care, hair care, detergent powder, cold drinks, toothpaste and packaged food	• Greater choice to the customers • Product customization, • Global quality standards • Supply chain networks
5	Pharmaceuticals • Pfizer Inc., Merck Inc, Mylan Inc., and Abbott Lab.	• Manufacturing of branded generics • Healthcare equipment • Joint manufacturing and marketing drugs • Clinical trial and research	• Employment generation • Over the counter drug market • development and manufacturing of vaccines
6	Consultancy • Counterpoint Consultants (India)	• Solution designing • Project management	• Promotion of outsourcing • Hires local workforce

India's gains from the American investment are varied. The prominent among them are

- These establishments provide employment to a diverse local workforce with improvement in wages and working conditions. The American investment in the IT sector has significantly increased employment opportunities in India. Microsoft Corporation (India) Private Limited was one of the first foreign companies to set up base in India's IT space. It set up its operations in 1990 and employed 6931 persons in 2015.[81] Companies such as Dell India have set up an assembling and R&D centre in India in addition to captive Business Process Outsourcing (BPO), sales and marketing, financial services and analytics, and software services. Dell currently employs about 27,000 people in India, about 23,000 of whom are associated with the company's services business.[82] In the banking sector, both the banking and the non-banking segments provide employment. In case of American banks, employment has been particularly high in sourcing operations, and one-third of the global workforce of an American offshoring unit is employed in India. Consulting firms, namely, PricewaterhouseCoopers Private Limited (PwC), KPMG India, Ernst&Young Private Limited (E&Y) and Deloitte Touche Tomhatsu India Private Limited, together account for approximately 37,000 employees across India. They operate under a slew of verticals such

---

[81] http://economictimes.indiatimes.com/slideshows/work-career/11-best-tech-workplaces-in-india-for-2015/microsoft-india-rank-20/slideshow/48064953.cms accessed on 5 September 2016.

[82] Adith Charlie, Dell can run global businesses out of India http://www.thehindubusinessline.com/info-tech/dell-can-run-global-businesses-out-of-india/article7024783.eceMarch 23, 2015 accessed on 5 September 2016.

as accountancy, auditing and tax. In this sector, there has been significant knowledge transmission from the home to the host country in the form of advanced software, and internal training programmes on research and communication skills. Companies in the FMCG segment have also invested in supply chain management to reach deeper into the rural market. Such companies provide employment to several thousand people. American Tower Corporation (ATC) India, a leading wireless infrastructure provider was established in 2007 in India and is mainly into construction of telecom towers. As majority of its activities takes place at the non-urban level, hence, the impact is the most at the village level through creation of bulk jobs.[83]

• They bring in the latest technology as well as capital— Operations of American banks have also facilitated transmission of technology. They have helped in laying the foundation for the Indian software industry. American investment has provided tremendous technological boost to the IT industry. American companies in the auto-component sector and automobile manufacturing companies have brought in latest technologies promoting conditions such as optimum cooling of engines, lowering noise levels and increasing fuel economy.

• Create the possibility of manufacturing for export market—The purpose of foreign direct investment is to increase production and maintain quality of product. The ample production help satisfy the domestic needs, and with the maintenance of quality also help maintain and

---

[83] Impact of American FDI in India, 15 May, 2015, http://www.ideasforindia. in/article.aspx?article_id=1451#sthash.yFykeLzp.dpuf accessed on 17 September 2016.

improve the standard of living of the people. The high levels of quantity and quality of production create the opportunities for export which ultimately would lead to increase in Indian exports. FDI can lead to vertical export expansion as well as horizontal export diversification.

- They help in maintenance of global quality standards of the products and services. The American companies such as Procter and Gamble, Amway bring in market the Fast Moving Consumer Goods such as hair care, skin care products, cold drinks, tooth paste, packed food, soaps and detergents etc. They sell variety of products and also are interested in customisation of products according to customer demand. These companies ensure the global standards of quality and operate with the help of supply chain networks. In this way they are successful in attracting wide range of customers and also provide employment to large number of people.

- Help in the improvement of HR skills—American companies investing in India are dependent primarily on the local workforce. For improving efficiency of Human Resource Departments, use of technology is utmost essential. US companies make the Indian workforce's easy access to the system of HR maintenance with the use of Technology, thus help in the improvement of HR skills. The American companies also take initiative to help upgrading the HR skills by providing advanced software and organizing training programmes.

- Establish the Research and Development Centres. Many American firms have set up their R&D centres in India. For example, Texas Instruments set up its R&D facility in 1985. In 1998, Microsoft set up Microsoft India

Development Centre (MSIDC) in Hyderabad, its second software development centre outside the US, leading the way for other such companies in the city. This has expanded to become one of Microsoft Corporation's largest R&D centres outside its headquarters in Redmond[84] In the pharmaceutical segment, US companies are engaged in R&D and clinical trials. Perrigo India initially focused on supporting global sourcing of active pharmaceutical ingredients. Gradually, they entered into the areas of formulation R&D, analytical R&D, quality assurance, external auditing and sourcing. US pharmaceutical companies have also made forays into the niche segment of stem cell research. For instance, StemCyte India Therapeutics Private Limited (SCITPL) is a joint venture between StemCyte Inc. (US), Apollo Hospital Enterprises Limited and Cadila Pharmaceuticals Limited. US pharmaceutical research organisations such as Quintiles India, Omnicare Inc. and Pharma-Olam International are conducting clinical trials in India.[85]

Further American companies in India undertake various CSR activities which include

- Significant employment generation for local workforce and their training
- Strictly following the environmental norms
- Maintaining safety standards and organising training for the same
- Employees of these companies teach at the local schools

---

[84] Ibid.
[85] Ibid.

- Donations and charities
- Partnership with NGOS
- Investments in Welfare promoting funds.

The report published by Academic Foundation, New Delhi in 2014, "Impact of American Investment in India" by Saon Ray, Smita Miglani and Neha Malik, also takes a brief review of companies with a significant presence in India and also companies with a negligible presence in India.

Companies with a Presence in India

1. General Electric (GE), operates in several segments such as energy, health care, aviation and transportation. This firm manages its health care manufacturing and renewable energy segment via joint ventures with Indian entities. It employs 15,000 people in the country of which about 4,000-5,000 are in its R&D centre. This centre caters to global needs and is involved in developing cutting edge products. About 10-15 per cent of manufactured products are exported from India.

2. International Paper is a US manufacturer of paper and packaging products and entered the Indian market in 2011. It is a 100 per cent subsidiary of the US parent. Some benefits of the investment have been in the form of significant technology spill over from the US parent in terms of improving the strength and quality of paper. The company is also looking ahead to setting up a Greenfield project for 'craft' paper.

3. Huber is, a US company, in the business of chemicals and additives in India. It started its operations as a joint venture in 1991 and became a 100 per cent owned company in

the year 1994, when it set up a manufacturing facility in Gujarat. The company supplies to the oral care, paints and coatings, beverage (fruit juices and jams), and paper industries. Companies such as Colgate Palmolive India Limited, Unilever and GlaxoSmithKline Pharmaceuticals Limited (GSK) are their customers. About 55 per cent of its manufactured products are exported to the South East, Middle East, Egypt, Thailand, Vietnam and Turkey.

Companies with Negligible Presence/Prospective Plans

1. PayPal Inc. is a US e-commerce business-based service allowing payments and money transfers without sharing financial information. They have established an offshore office in India, which employs around 100 people. This office and its operations are essentially aimed at providing customer support in order to maintain their existing products.

2. Millennial Media Inc. is a leading American independent mobile advertising and data platform powering the app economy. They have a presence in India but this remains negligible due to lack of a well-developed market in the absence of a large base of smart phone users.

3. William Scotsman Inc. is a US company that makes, leases, sells and manages mobile offices and is considering the Indian market as they see a large demand for their products, especially in the construction sector. The company is currently in the phase of analysing the logistics of providing modular spaces in India. In addition, they also aim to start a pilot project in the suburbs of Mumbai that will allow them to study the feasibility of entering the Indian market.

4. Counterpoint Consultants (India) is a provider of
    enterprise software solutions. It provides advisory
    services such as vendor selection and management and
    programme remediation for offshoring programmes.
    The company has made no significant investments in
    India but hires a local workforce to work at their head
    office in Virginia (USA). The reason is the absence of a
    large market in India for their cloud and mobile-based
    business automation solutions.

The Problems Faced by American Companies

1. Problems related with Taxation and regulatory procedures:
    American companies in the IT sector primarily face
    problems with the taxation policies and the regulatory
    procedures of the Government of India. There are
    concerns both with the indirect taxation regarding service
    tax refund procedures, and in the direct taxation regarding
    corporate tax collection procedures. The companies face
    problems because of the lack of clarity regarding the
    provisions, arbitrary or confusing regulations regarding
    taxable income. This problem is creating a major hurdle
    in investment and transfer of technology.

2. In the banking sector, the American banks face problems
    because of RBI requirement to open branches even in
    the smaller towns to facilitate their financial inclusion.
    But the question of sustainability of these banks is a
    major issue as these banks do not get the required skill
    workforce in the smaller towns. Also there are different
    rules and procedures regarding audit and compliances of
    these banks and the Indian Banks. Different regulatory
    concerns on the one hand and the infrastructural and
    logistic requirements including internet facilities on

the other hand create problems in the working of these banks.

3. Current regulatory structure and pricing mechanism is a problem even for the pharmaceutical sector in India. Delays in the issuing of licences, non-availability of animals for laboratory research, the documentation requirements which may be excessive sometimes, lack of incentives for manufacturing of medical devices in India and the lack of coordination in the different departments of the Government are the major problems faced by the American investors in pharmaceutical sector.

4. Another major problem that the investor face is the different laws existing at the Centre and State level due to federal structure and requirement of compliance to the both Central and the State laws. This may sometimes act as a major hurdle for the American investors.

To conclude, the contribution of American investment is enormous to the economic growth of India. India's high skilled workforce and success in technological advancement have made India an advantageous location for US firms for the purpose of research and innovation. This trend towards partnership between India and US is very clearly visible in information technology sector and pharmaceutical sector. India's initiative for educational reforms in order to make the education system globally competent has provided additional opportunities for US to invest in Indian economy. The dramatic increase in India-US economic interaction initially was possible because of active interests of both the Governments in facilitating bilateral investments and trade flows. Today, it is largely in the hands of private sectors of both the countries. Economic engagement is also emerging as a motivation and opportunity for closer and broader strategic partnership between the two nations. India, an emerging power is seeking its rightful place in the global set up and engagement with US is essential to achieve this goal.

CHAPTER 5

Indian Presence in US

After India adopted economic reforms in 1991, India's investments abroad began to increase. In the last decade it has increased manifold. The accelerated Investment is the result of several factors. By advancing trade relations with different countries, Indian companies are in a better negotiable position. Favourable environment to business at domestic and international level, the large talent pool of India and increasing ease to do business have contributed the investments flows to India and from India, thus strengthening India's relations with the outside world. There is a major change in the investment policy of India. In the decades of cold war, India's major investments were in the developing nations—in line with the policy of South-South cooperation. However in the new millennium, India has increasingly focused its attention on highly developed economies—beginning with the "Look East" policy and now moving closer to developed world by building economic engagement with US.

After India's economic reforms, the Indian presence in US increased considerably. Majority of Indians going to America fall in the category of highly skilled knowledge workers and have emerged as the very productive segment of US population. The growing number of Indian have contributed in the economic growth of US. Before the emergence of powerful IT industry, in 1960s and 70s, Indian professionals in medicine, Engineering and Law had established themselves in US and have secured the position of respect in American society. Today, due to higher educational qualifications of Indians particularly in Engineering and IT, they have occupied managerial and professional positions. In IT industry, more than 300000 Indian Americans work and there are around 700 Indian owned companies. Due to the pressure from Indian IT companies in US, the number of visas approved by Congress has been increased and there is liberalization of H1-B visa conditions. Indian expertise in the field of Bio technology has facilitated their entry in various sensitive fields. Indian-Americans who are Engineers, Scientists, and Technical experts work in NASA, Boing, and also nuclear and other laboratories. Apart from that, many of them are in technical, sales and service sectors and the less educated are working as skilled labourers. In early 1990s, many of the Indians in the field of IT began to settle in US and established their own companies.

Indian-Americans, who account for only about 1 percent of the US population, have ascended to a disproportionately influential position in American medicine, academia, corporations and especially the high-tech sector. The San Jose Mercury News reported in late November that Asian-Americans (which include Indians) comprise more than one-half (52 percent) of the technology workforce in the Bay Area. Between 2000 and 2010 the Asian proportion of tech workers jumped from 39 percent to 52 percent.[86] According

---

[86] Palash Ghosh, "The Rise of Indian-Americans in US Business" [Infographic] http://www.ibtimes.com/rise-indian-americans-u-s-business-infographic-1560450, 03/10/2014, accessed on 21 September 2016.

to Economic Times (report 21st Sept 2015) the Indian Tech industry created 411000 jobs in the US economy and contributed to more than $375 million to the US treasury between fiscal year 2011 to 2015. Indian talent also helped the US firms to improve their global market share by providing cost effective solutions. California, Texas, Illinois, New Jersey and New York are the top five American states where Indian IT companies have supported direct jobs. According to the report "Indian tech industry paid over $20 billion in taxes to the US treasury between FY 2011 to FY 2015".

The Socio-Cultural Impact

The Indo-American community is considered to be the socially prestigious community in US. It is due to their high educational profile, hard-working nature, knowledge of English and general commitment to rules and regulations and respect for democracy as a whole. They are considered to have easy adaptability to foreign culture. Indian diversity of religion, language and culture also finds its presence in US and seem to preserve their own traditions by establishing their own socio-cultural organizations and celebrating their national function and festivals. The religious centres of different religions have also been established carrying out cultural, social, educational, and charitable activities. Moreover professional organizations also exist such as Indo-American Chamber of Commerce, Indo-US entrepreneurs, Network of Indian Professionals, etc. which function as umbrella organizations.

Indians also comprise a significant voting and political force. There are many organizations in US, such as, Indian-American forum for political education, India Abroad

Centre for Political Awareness, US-India Business Council and such others which effectively raise the issues concerning Indian-Americans and issues related with the relations between India and US. Indian-Americans have also acted as the back bone of Indo-US nuclear deal. Their active presence helps in creating favourable environment for positive relationship between India and US. Indian Americans who are the politically active community plays an important role in opinion building on current issues and act as important pressuring agents in the decision making process. In Congress, Indian American representatives have been elected and have made their present felt by defeating anti-India legislations in case of nuclear issues and advocated India's stand in its conflict with Pakistan during Kargil episode and later other conflicting areas. This community is also the strong supporter of India's demand for permanent membership of United Nation's Security Council in US.

The Business Investments

During the period 2004-2009, 90 Indian companies started 127 new ventures by constructing new facilities in USA.[87] This type of foreign direct investment is called as Greenfield investment when a parent company begins a new venture by constructing new facilities in a country outside of where the company is headquartered.[88]

In addition to the construction of new production facilities, these projects can also include the building of new distribution hubs, offices and living quarters. Such investments provide the highest degree of control for the sponsoring company.

---

[87] Surbhi Bhatia "India Inc Creates Jobs in the US" http://epaper. timesofindia.com/ accessed on 5 September 2016.

[88] www.investopedia.com/terms/g/greenfield.asp accessed on 22 September 2016.

Top Ten US Sectors Receiving
Greenfield Investments from India[89]

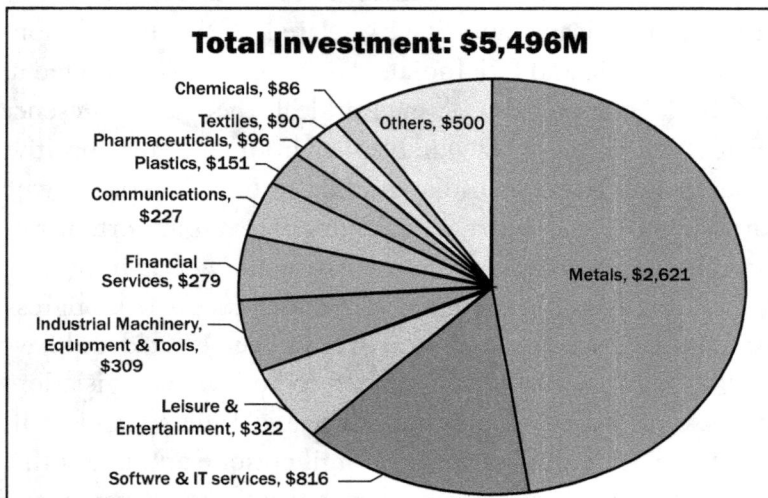

Total Investment: $5,496M

Chemicals, $86
Textiles, $90
Pharmaceuticals, $96
Plastics, $151
Communications, $227
Financial Services, $279
Industrial Machinery, Equipment & Tools, $309
Leisure & Entertainment, $322
Softwre & IT services, $816
Others, $500
Metals, $2,621

This investment was worth $5.5 billion, and created 16,576 jobs in the United States. The top three destination states for Greenfield investments were Minnesota, Virginia, and Texas, in that order. However, the top three states in terms of jobs created were Ohio, Texas, and California. The five US industrial sectors that received the most greenfield investment were Metals; Software & IT Services; Leisure & Entertainment; industrial machinery, equipment & tools; and financial services, accounting for almost 80% of total greenfield investment in the United States. It is noteworthy that the software and IT services sector received less than 15% of total investment, and the bulk of investments went into mining, manufacturing, and other industries.[90]

[89] Vinod K. Jain and Kamlesh Jain, "How America Benefits from Economic Engagement with India" India-US World Affairs Institute, Inc. June 2010, www.india-us.org, accessed on 22 September 2016.

[90] Surbhi Bhatia "India INC Creates Jobs in the US" http://epaper. timesofindia.com/ accessed on 5 September 2016.

India's Mergers and Acquisitions in the United States

During 2004-2009, 239 Indian companies made 372 acquisitions in the United States. The total value of the 267 acquisitions was $21 billion, or $78.7 million per acquisition. Five states that attracted the most M&A investments from Indian companies accounted for 75% of total deal value: Georgia, New Jersey, Michigan, California, and Texas. The five leading US sectors receiving M&A investments from India were: Manufacturing; IT & IT Enabled Services; Biotech, Chemicals & Pharmaceuticals; Automotive; and Telecom—for a total of 83% of total deal value. The bulk of M&A investments by India Inc. in the United States were in manufacturing and other industrial sectors, rather than in services for which India is well known.[91]

There are currently almost 10,000 Indian American owners of hotels/motels in the United States, who together own over 21,000 hotels with 1.8 million guest rooms and property valued at $129 billion. They employ 578,600 workers. India has had the largest number of foreign students in the United States among all countries of origin for eight years in a row. In 2008, there were 94,563 students from India whose net contribution to the US economy was $2.39 billion.[92]

Indian Investments in US

Indian firms are investing billions of dollars in US. The three important States with the largest FDI from India are Texas, Pennsylvania and Minnesota creating over 12000 local jobs. According to a survey by the Confederation of Indian industry and Grant Thornton, 100 firms have made

---

[91] ibid.

[92] ibid.

15 billion dollars' worth of tangible investments across 35 States, creating more than 91000 American jobs. The largest number of jobs were created in New Jersey–9278, California–8937 and Texas–6230.[93]

Indian FDI in the U.S. more than doubled between 2010 and 2015

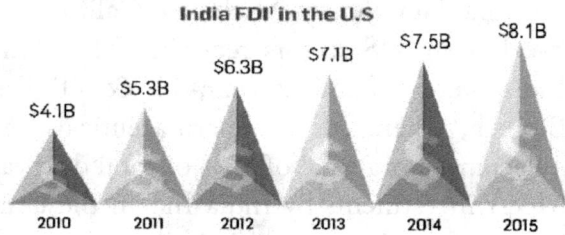

India FDI' in the U.S

2010	2011	2012	2013	2014	2015
$4.1B	$5.3B	$6.3B	$7.1B	$7.5B	$8.1B

The U.S. FDI' in India

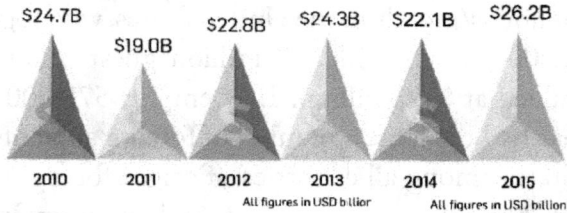

2010	2011	2012	2013	2014	2015
$24.7B	$19.0B	$22.8B	$24.3B	$22.1B	$26.2B

All figures in USD billion   All figures in USD billion

Notes: 'Foreign Direct Investment is an investment in a business of a foreign country, FDI is taken as direct investment position on a historic cost basis
Source: Bureau of Economic Analysis, U.S. Department of Commerce. Zinnov Analysis

Source: Library of USIS

More than one third of the money coming into the US is going to the IT sector. The other industries receiving major investment include life science, pharmaceuticals, health care, mining, material etc. In the last five years, India has emerged as the fourth fastest source of FDI in the US. 362 investment projects have been announced by Indian firms between

---

[93] Nate Schlabach, "Indian Companies investing billions across the US", asiamattersforamerica.org, August 6, 2015 accessed on 26 September 2016.

January 2003 and October 2014.[94] According to the survey undertaken by the Confederation of Indian Industry, the presence of Indian companies in US is constantly growing. Indian companies have their presence in all 50 States of US.[95]

INDIAN COMPANIES OPERATIONS IN THE U.S

- $15.3 billion of tangible investments made
- 91,000 jobs created
- 84.5% of companies plan to make further investments in next 5 years
- 90% of companies plan to hire more workers locally in next 5 years

INDUSTRY DIVERSIFICATION

IT & Telecom - 40%
Pharmaceuticals & Health Care - 14%
Mining & Manufacturing - 14%
Financial Services - 6%
Design, Engineering & Construction - 5%
Media & Entertainment - 5%
Other - 4%
Automotive - 4%
Energy - 4%
Tourism & Hospitality - 2%
Food & Agriculture - 2%

Refer footnote 96

[94] ibid.

[95] Mohul Ghosh, "Indian Companies Invested $17B in USA, Generated 81000 Jobs!" http://trak.in/tags/business/2014/03/28/indian-investment-fdi-usa/ accessed on 5 September 2016.

[96] http://trendline.dcrworkforce.com/indian-companies-account-for-thousands-of-us-jobs.html#sthash.UajtSNp4.dpuf, accessed on 5 September 2016.

Five States—New Jersey, California, New York, Pennsylvania and Illinois have the highest concentration of Indian Companies. 84.5% of the Indian companies plan to make more "long term investments" in the US and 90% of these companies plan to hire locally for their businesses in the next five years.[97]

Texas, Pennsylvania, Minnesota, New York and New Jersey are the beneficiaries of highest Indian FDI.

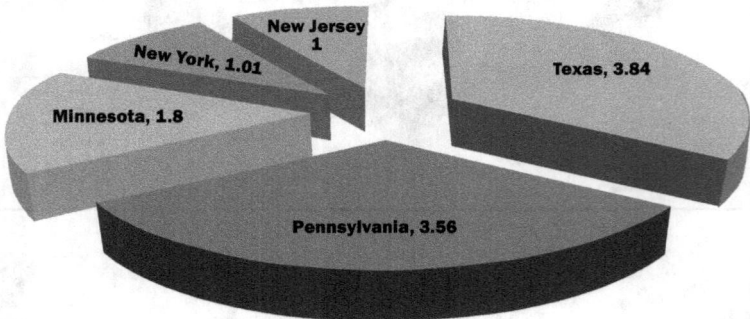

Indian companies have created highest number of jobs in New Jersey, California, Texas, Illinois and New York.[98]

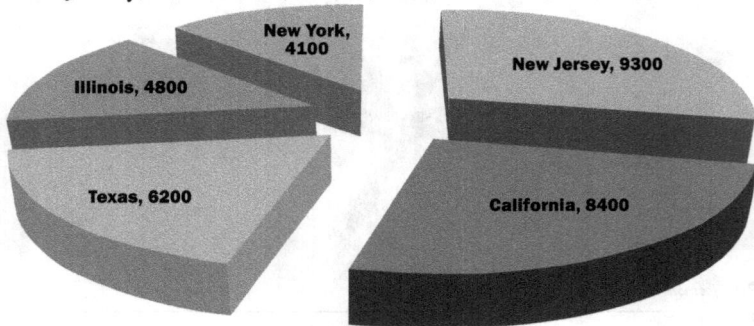

---

[97] Vaishnavi Kanekar, "Indian Businesses Invested Over ₹ 97,000 Cr in US, Create 91,000 Jobs For Americans!" http://trak.in/tags/business/2015/07/17/indian-businesses-invested-in-us-create-91000-jobs-americans/ accessed on 25 March 2016.

[98] Ibid.

Top 25 States with Largest Indian Investment [99]

Sl. No.	Name of the State	Total Volume of Investment($)	Number of Indian Companies Present in the State	Total No. of Jobs Created
1	Texas	3,847,854,973	17	6,230
2	Pennsylvania	3,563,546,300	20	3,370
3	Minnesota	1.804,000,000	6	2,454
4	New York	1.011,030,333	23	4,134
5	New Jersey	1,004,940,346	36	9,278
6	Massachusetts	9352,48,333	14	2,137
7	Georgia	3435,98,500	16	4,021
8	Louisiana	3350,00,000	7	359
9	Arkansas	3045,00,000	6	1,184
10	California	2959,72,543	30	8,397
11	Washington	2419,00,000	10	3,040
12	North Carolina	2369,70,000	8	2,579
13	Kentucky	2250,00,000	6	1,808
14	Wisconsin	1590,00,000	8	1,243
15	Illinois	1586,76,000	18	4,779
16	Kansas	1130,00,000	5	320
17	Maryland	1042,75,000	11	830
18	Virginia	1034,10,500	12	1,431
19	Lowa	1000,30,000	6	576
20	Ohio	529,65,769	18	3,759
21	Missouri	450,00,000	7	966
22	Tennessee	400,00,000	6	690
23	Michigan	389,03,466	18	3,057
24	Oregon	250,00,000	5	612
25	Indiana	250,00,000	5	766

[99] "Indian Roots, American Soil, A survey of Indian companies' state-by-state operations in the United States", http://online.wsj.com/public/resources/documents/CIIReport.pdf, accessed on 27 March 2016.

Sector-wise Investment by Indian Companies in Top 25 States of USA

Sl. No.	Name of the State	IT and Telecom	Design, Engineering Construction	Energy	Life Science Pharma Health Care	Media Entertainment	Mining Material Manufacturing	Financial Service	Tourism Hospitality	Automotive	Food Agriculture	Other
1	Texas	64%	12%	6%	6%	6%	6%	---	---	---	---	---
2	Pennsylvania	60%	---	5%	25%	---	10%	---	---	---	---	---
3	Minnesota	83%	---	---	---	---	17%	---	---	---	---	---
4	New York	44%	---	---	4%	4%	13%	26%	9%	---	---	---
5	New Jersey	53%	3%	---	25%	5%	5%	3%	---	3%	3%	---
6	Massachusetts	50%	7%	---	15%	7%	7%	---	7%	---	---	7%
7	Georgia	63%	---	---	13%	---	13%	---	---	---	6%	6%
8	Louisiana	57%	---	---	29%	---	14%	---	---	---	---	---
9	Arkansas	83%	---	---	---	---	17%	---	---	---	---	---
10	California	47%	10%	---	13%	10%	7%	3%	3%	---	3%	3%
11	Washington	60%	---	---	30%	---	10%	---	---	---	---	---
12	North Carolina	75%	---	---	13%	---	---	---	---	13%	---	---
13	Kentucky	67%	---	---	---	---	33%	---	---	---	---	---
14	Wisconsin	63%	12%	---	25%	---	---	---	---	---	---	---
15	Illinois	61%	11%	6%	11%	---	6%	6%	---	---	---	---
16	Kansas	80%	---	---	---	---	20%	---	---	---	---	---
17	Maryland	64%	---	---	27%	---	---	---	---	---	27%	---
18	Virginia	75%	17%	---	8%	---	8%	---	---	---	---	8%
19	Lowa	50%	17%	---	17%	---	17%	---	---	---	---	---
20	Ohio	56%	6%	---	6%	---	28%	---	---	6%	---	---
21	Missouri	71%	---	---	29%	---	---	---	---	---	---	---
22	Tennessee	67%	---	---	17%	---	17%	---	---	---	---	---
23	Michigan	50%	17%	6%	11%	---	11%	---	---	6%	---	---
24	Oregon	80%	---	---	---	---	20%	---	---	---	---	---
25	Indiana	60%	---	---	20%	---	20%	---	---	---	---	---

The above table shows the sector wise investment of the Indian Companies in top 25 States in USA. Indian companies have their maximum investment in IT and Telecom sector in all 25 state which are top in the list of States having maximum Indian investment in US. The other sectors in which Indian companies have investment is:

1. In mining, material and manufacturing sector, in 21 States, Indian companies have the investment.
2. Life Science, Pharma and Health care. In this sector, in 20 States, Indian companies have good amount of investment.
3. In 9 States, Indian companies have investment in design, engineering and construction sector.
4. In 5 States, Indian companies have investment in media and entertainment sector
5. In 4 States, Indian companies have investment in energy, financial services, food and agriculture and automotive sectors.
6. In 3 States, Indian companies have investment in tourism sector.

Looking at the destination of these FDIs, IT/Knowledge sector remains the most invested sector with 40% of the investments going into it.

Sector-wise split of Indian companies in the US

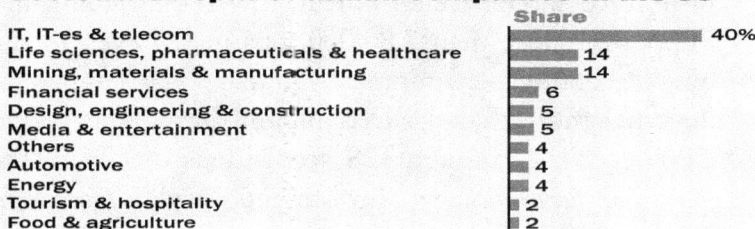

Sector	Share
IT, IT-es & telecom	40%
Life sciences, pharmaceuticals & healthcare	14
Mining, materials & manufacturing	14
Financial services	6
Design, engineering & construction	5
Media & entertainment	5
Others	4
Automotive	4
Energy	4
Tourism & hospitality	2
Food & agriculture	2

Refer footnote 100

[100] "Indian companies are spending billions and boosting jobs in these US states" http://qz.com/455573/indian-companies-are-spending-billions-and-boosting-jobs-in-these-us-states/ accessed on 25 March 2016.

There are various important factors driving Indo-US relations:

1. Globalization has led to the economic integration of the world. As a result the relationship between consumer/client and producer/service provider has changed dramatically. The increased network of transportation and communication and the extensive use of technology has helped to bridge the gap in the time zones of different nations. This particularly facilitates the relationship between India and US. The relationship between consumer/client and producer/service provider can be more satisfactory due to 9 to12 hours of time difference between India and US which allows extended work day and help reduce time for US clients. Indian companies have been facilitated as they are able to create onsite jobs and also extend indirect support as people can operate from India for US companies.

2. Indian companies support US employment scenario by creating employment in US. This was especially crucial during recession when Indian companies were able to add jobs and hire local in the US rather than reducing workforce. Aegis, Genpact, HCL, Mind Tree and TCS are the important companies which in fact increased US workforce in their establishment. Thus Indian companies supported more than 2,80,000 jobs in US even in the weak economic environment. Indian Tech companies invested more than USD 5 billion during the period 2007 to 2011, through 128 acquisitions in US. In the period of recession, these investments saved thousands of jobs in the US.[101]

---

[101] "Indian Tech Industry in the US—A Contribution Review", NASSCOM, New Delhi, 2012 https://www.indianembassy.org/pdf/News_File_1890. pdf accessed on 25 March 2016.

3. It is seen that Indian companies are engaged in increasing direct employment across all States in US. Direct employment refers to the jobs which are created at the client location and development centres. 3 out of every 4 jobs supported by Indian companies are constituted by local in US.[102]

4. For every 1 direct job, approximately 1.6 indirect jobs are supported. These direct jobs support indirect jobs covering supplier industry such as logistics, travel, courier, telecom, computer hardware and re-spending industry covering retail, utility, travel, hospitality, Pharma, IT, etc. About 1,75,000 indirect jobs are supported by Indian companies.[103]

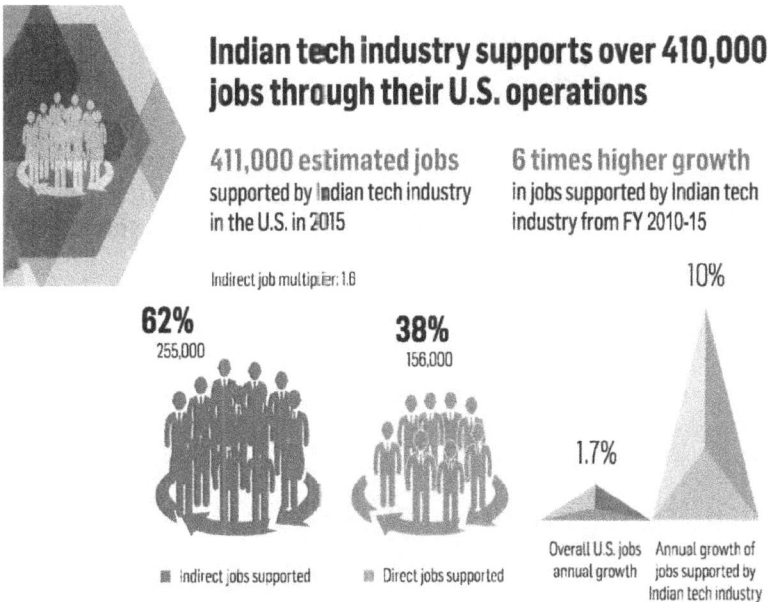

Indian tech industry supports over 410,000 jobs through their U.S. operations

411,000 estimated jobs supported by Indian tech industry in the U.S. in 2015

6 times higher growth in jobs supported by Indian tech industry from FY 2010-15

Indirect job multiplier: 1.6

62% 255,000

38% 156,000

10%

1.7%

Overall U.S. jobs annual growth

Annual growth of jobs supported by Indian tech industry

■ Indirect jobs supported   ■ Direct jobs supported

---

[102] Ibid.
[103] Ibid.

Jobs Supported in the U.S.

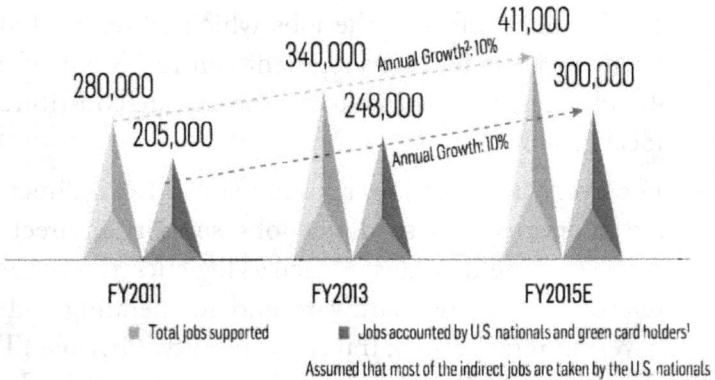

411,000

340,000 Annual Growth²: 10%

280,000

300,000

248,000

205,000

Annual Growth: 10%

FY2011   FY2013   FY2015E

■ Total jobs supported   ■ Jobs accounted by U S nationals and green card holders¹

Assumed that most of the indirect jobs are taken by the U.S. nationals

Notes: ¹Includes U.S citizenship/US passport holders
      ² Refers to compounded annual growth rate; FY refers to Oct-Sep period

Source: Library of USIS

5. Indian Tech industry has paid more than USD 22.5 billion in taxes to the US treasury.[104]

Indian tech industry paid over USD 20 billion in taxes to the U.S. treasury between FY2011 to FY2015E

Total Taxes¹ Paid in the U.S.

USD 22.5 billion
Total Taxes Paid (FY2011-15E)

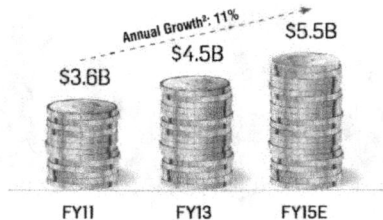

Annual Growth²: 11%

$5.5B

$4.5B

$3.6B

FY11   FY13   FY15E

---

[104] http://thebricspost.com/indian-tech-firms-paid-22-5bn-in-taxes-in-us-from-2011-15/#.VwvB96R942w accessed on 25 March 2016.

Social Security Contribution in the U.S.

USD 6.6 billion
Total Social Security
Contribution (FY2011-15E)

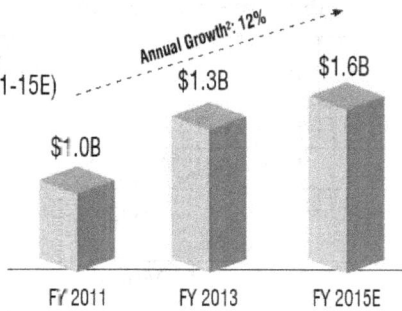

Annual Growth²: 12%

$1.0B

$1.3B

$1.6B

FY 2011   FY 2013   FY 2015E

Notes: ¹ Includes Income, payroll and all other taxes
² Refers to compounded annual growth rate
Source: NASSCOM Member Survey: Zinnov Analysis

All figures in USD billion

6. Indian tech industry contributed nearly 411,000 jobs to the US economy this year and $20 billion in taxes between 2011-15 when American firms leveraged Indian talent to provide innovative and cost-competitive solutions to boost their global market share. The NASSCOM said Indian tech industry contributed more than $375 million to the US Treasury between fiscal year 2011-2015, and also helped America secure its borders. "Leveraging Indian talent, American firms have been able to bring better, innovative, cost-competitive solutions that have helped improve their global market share and bring products with shorter production cycles." These benefits included $2 billion in investments, hundreds of thousands of new jobs for Americans, $20 billion in taxes, and more than 120,000 American lives touched through philanthropic work supported by Indian organizations.[105]

[105] http://timesofindia.indiatimes.com/tech/jobs/Indian-IT-supports-over-411000-jobs-in-US-Nasscom/articleshow/49047161.cms, accessed on 25 March 2016.

Several Indian Companies have their Establishment in Various States of US

Sl. No.	States	The Companies having Operations
1	California	TCS, HCL, Wipro, Infosys, Gen pact, UST Global
2	Michigan	TCS, HCL, Wipro, Infosys, Gen Pact, Aditya Birla
3	New Jersey	TCS, HCL, Wipro, Infosys, Gen Pact, Aditya Birla, EXL
4	Texas	TCS, HCL, Wipro, Infosys, EXL, UST Global, Aditya Birla, Aegis
5	Illinois	TCS, HCL, Wipro, Infosys, Gen Pact, Infotech, Headstrong

These companies are playing a significant role such as

- Supporting research centres
- Research and development partnership
- Hiring Engineering graduates from the US universities
- Creating local BPO delivery centres.

7. As mentioned above, the Indian companies are also involved in the CSR (Corporate Social Responsibility) Activities. They include:

- Raising funds for charity
- Raising funds for breast-cancer research, for HIV/AIDS and health care programmes
- Raising funds Collection of school supplies, food items, clothing, writing material, etc.
- Enhancing employability and driving rural employment
- Generating environmental consciousness.

The significant Indian presence in various sectors in US and diversity of Indian companies' operations in US is indicative of the fact that, there is increasing demand for large and economically strong Indian diaspora. Due to the substantial role of Indian companies in investment and employment generation in US, economic engagement of India and US has become an important component of Indo-US bilateral relations.

CHAPTER 6

Inside Techdom

The relationship between Silicon Valley and India has greatly evolved over the years, from the Diaspora of Indian engineers hired by American technology companies to the outsourcing boom of remote Indian workers. The two tech hubs have shared an intimate relationship over many decades that has resulted in innovation for both sides. India is on the world's stage with big bets from Silicon Valley and global investors in its start-up sector. In fact, venture capital investment in India hit a record high with $1.44 billion as of October— exceeding the $1.17 billion invested in all of 2014. Indian IT industry representative NASSCOM has predicted that Indian startups are on track to garner $5 billion by the end of 2015.[106] Indian companies have established themselves in the US covering a wide segment of industries in several States of the United States of America.[107] This has growing impact on the US economy over a period of time. The IT Sector played an important role by being in the forefront of Indian Investment development in the US IT Sector made

---

[106] Matthew Howard Promod Haque, Growing Up Together: The Next Evolution for the India-Silicon Valley Relationship JAN 5, 2016, http://www.recode.net/2016/1/5/11588452/growing-up-together-the-next-evolution-for-the-india-silicon-valley accessed on 25 March 2016.

[107] CIIStudy—Indian Companies growing impact on the US economy http://www.cii.in/PressreleasesDetail.aspx (July 15, 2015).

a remarkable success story by growing 30% annually for the last 30 years. It expanded in such a way that 2016 exports are projected close to $80 billion. India exports software services to more than 60 countries with two thirds to the United States, including half of all Fortune 500 companies.

Indian tech industry has produced a multi-fold impact on the U.S. economy

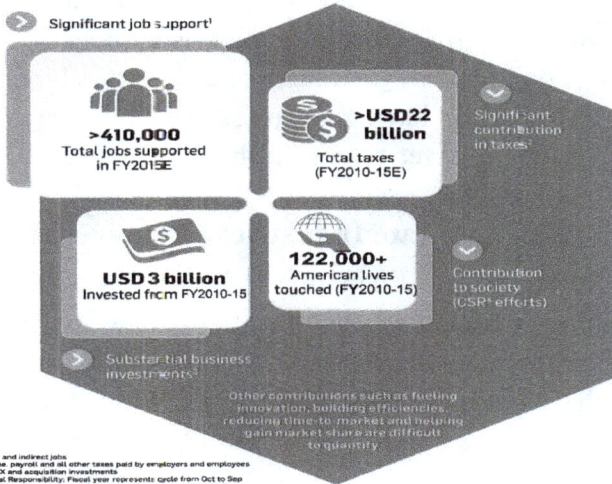

> Significant job support[1]

>410,000
Total jobs supported in FY2015E

>USD22 billion
Total taxes (FY2010-15E)

Significant contribution in taxes[2]

USD 3 billion
Invested from FY2010-15

122,000+
American lives touched (FY2010-15)

Contribution to society (CSR[4] efforts)

> Substantial business investments[3]

Other contributions such as fueling innovation, building efficiencies, reducing time-to-market and helping gain market share are difficult to quantify

Notes: [1]Includes direct and indirect jobs.
[2]Includes income, payroll and all other taxes paid by employers and employees
[3]Includes CAPEX and acquisition investments
[4]Corporate Social Responsibility; Fiscal year represents cycle from Oct to Sep

Source: Nehru Centre Library, Mumbai

The origin of Indian IT industry in US can be traced back to 1960s. In the latter half of 1960s, immigration of Indian Students to US was encouraged as a policy by US government. US immigration and nationality act was amended and the quota system depending on national origin for residency in US was abolished. This encouraged among all others the IIT students of India who had moved to US for their post-graduation to aspire for settling in US. This was also a time for massive development in the Electronics industry in US and these fresh, extremely talented Indian post-graduates were hired by the high technology companies in Silicon Valley, which was just emerging as Electronic Hub. Gradually more Indians started coming in large numbers for post-graduation and then for jobs. After the information technology revolution in India in late 80s, most of the students and job seekers moving to Silicon Valley were with the Computer Science background. With the development of internet technology newer entrepreneurial opportunities were created and even internet technology domain came to be dominated by the Indian technocrats. US educated Indian professionals having technical and managerial capabilities continued to get success in the Silicon Valley.

Indian Software Industries in the Decade of 90s

Driven by the Economic Policy change, liberalization and appreciation of quality of work done by Indian Engineers in the US; Indian software firms quickly moved up the value chain from performing low cost programing work to providing comprehensive e-software developing services from India to overseas clients. In the early stages, Government of India invested heavily in technical education by creating chain of elite technical and Management institutes at a vulnerable time when the world was facing a huge shortage of technical manpower.[108] This helped Indian firms to access a pool of English speaking well trained professionals, who could be sent to onsite clients' facilities in the US.

---

[108] Subash Bhatnagar, "India's Software Industry".
http://iimahd.ernet.in/~subhash/pdfs/Indian%20software%20industry.
pdf, accessed on 25 March 2016.

Arising out of this development, Indian professionals in the Silicon Valley built personal networks and valuable reputation during the early part of 1980s. These professionals offered a variety of software services to US Companies and in the process got a foot in the door of the expanding opportunity of outsourced IT work. Once the potential for software experts was demonstrated, Indian Government helped build a high speed data communication infrastructure. This allowed overseas Indians to return home and set up offshore sites for US clients. The Indian "brand" image for affordable speed and quality expanded considerably. Intense quality and productivity improvements built client value and today these companies deliver a wide range of software development tasks, as well as benefits in new service segments such as product design and information science (IS) outsourcing. Many Indian companies have met stringent certification requirements for quality standards in demand around the globe.[109] As we witness today new frontiers in Cyber Security, data protection, cloud computing are all moving to the top of the Agenda.

By 2000, Indian Engineers were at the helm of 972 Silicon Valley based technology companies, which accounted for approximately $5 billion in sales and 25811 jobs.[110] The proportion of Indian-founded startups in Silicon Valley startups has increased from 7% to 15.5% from 1999 to 2012. With Sundar Pichai, 43, being named chief executive officer

---

[109] Subash Bhatnagar, "India's Software Industry" Technology, Adaptation and Exports: How developing countries got it right by Ms. Vandana Chandra (Ed.) World Bank 2006.

[110] A. D'Costa, E. Sridharan, India in the Global Software Industry: Innovation, Firm Strategies and Development, Palgrave MacMillon, New York, 2004.

of Google today, and Satya Nadella heading Microsoft, Indians are now poised to dominate the upper echelons of the technology giants as well.[111]

The Indian Story in The Valley

1980s
Influx of software engineers who started going there for programming work

1990s
Entrepreneurial spirit palpable, and several Indians - Vinod Khosla, Kanwal Rekhi, Romesh Wadhwani - made significant amounts of money

They became venture capitalists and angel investors who founded another generation of companies led by Indians through the first decade of the millennium

Other Indians went on to become leaders in large companies

Late 2000
Indian entrepreneurial community swells in numbers

Network of investors, entrepreneurs and senior managers fuels growth in large companies

Present
Indians such as Sundar Pichai and Satya Nadella now lead top tech companies

Indians now the top entrepreneurial ethnic group in the Valley, starting more companies than the next four ethnic groups put together

16%
Share of new ventures of the total estimated to be started by Indians in the valley

Refer footnote 112

Success Stories

During the eighties and nineties, the image of India among our global peers, was one of a country, beset with poverty, expanding huge population and substandard manufactured products. However, due to the dramatic growth in the Indian Software Industry and growth of international Corporates

---

[111] Sunainaa Chadha, "More than just Pichai and Nadella: Indians now the biggest power players in Silicon Valley" Aug 12, 2015, http://www.firstpost.com/business/more-than-just-sundar-pichai-and-satya-nadella-indians-now-the-biggest-power-players-in-silicon-valley-2387058.html

[112] http://economictimes.indiatimes.com/tech/ites/how-long-will-it-be-before-indian-entrepreneurs-build-top-companies-out-of-silicon-valley/articleshow/48520411.cms accessed on 25 April 2016.

such as Infosys, Wipro, TCS, etc. India is viewed as a fountainhead of talent, techno savvy corporates employing outstanding professionals. Certain parts of India are beset with problems of poor infrastructure and other issues connected with food distribution.[113]

Mr. R. Chandrashekhar, President, NASSCOM, has stated in a report that Indo-US Bilateral Trade, since 2012 has crossed the US $100 Billion mark and is strategically poised to cross the US $100 Billion mark, aiming to reach the goal of US $500 Billion. American businesses have responded with enthusiasm to Prime Minister Modi's pledge of "less red tape and more red carpet" for US investment and trade with India. American firms are being encouraged to combine Information Technologies and know-how with Indian IT businesses to expand Cellular Phone and internet services, implement E-Governance initiates and pursue the visions for Smart Cities and connecting a Digital India of over 6000 villages.

According to Mr. Harish Mehta (former NASSCOM Chairman), one of the hallmarks of Indo-IS Economic Engagement is the exchange of specialized knowledge and human talent. Many US organizations send high skilled Americans to India to manage investments and operations; install and service specialized equipment; and assist with manufacturing facilities, commercial aircraft, software and other products made in USA. This sharing of capital, talent and energy works in other directions too.

---

[113] Contributions of India's Tech Industry to the US economy. http://www.nasscom.in/contributions india%E2%80%99s-tech-industry-us-economy, accessed on 25 February, 2016.

Indian FDI in the US more than doubled between 2009 and 2015. The Indian Technology Industry alone invested over US $3 billion and paid over US $20 billion in US Federal State and local taxes—while supporting approximately 410,000 jobs in America. NASSCOM members also supported many initiatives in the US education, capacity building, health care and other philanthropic areas. Many of these programs are focused on STEM education for Americans to help address a chronic shortage of IT Specialists to meet the fast growing needs of US business, government and not for profit sectors.

Mr. Ashank Desai, Chairman of MASTEK said that there is much more to what the IT Sector brings to the table. One should also consider the Economic Value of the operational support provided to over 90 percent of Fortune 500 firms and thousands of other American businesses. NASSCOM study shows that Indian IT firms make their US customers more innovative, competitive, and primed for new market opportunities and eager to expand jobs. American customers benefitting from these services encompass every corner of commerce and size of business.

The two way flow of investments and intellectual talent is central to the growing commercial and strategic relationships between India and the US. It is not about one nation taking unfair advantage of the other; it is about moving forward together to improve economies, opportunities and quality of life for citizens of both nations. This is a unique partnership between the world's oldest and largest democracies.[114]

---

[114] Personal interview with Mr. Harish Mehta, former Chairman of NASSCOM, May 3 2016 and Meeting with Mr. Ashank Desai and Meeting with R. Chandrasekhar, President, NASSCOM.

By 2015 around 15% startups were founded by Indians. A very strong educational base of Indians and the high technical skills, strong entrepreneurial skills and work ethics are the key reasons for the success of Indians in Silicon Valley. Indians are not only in the top executive position but 89000 Indians live in the Silicon Valley. Nearly 16% of start-ups in Silicon Valley had an Indian co-founder even though Indians represented just 6% of the region's population. The figure for Indian start-ups is even higher in some areas, such as business software.[115]

Twelve technologies can empower India in the next decade

Digitising life and work		Mobile Internet	Inexpensive and increasingly capable mobile devices and Internet connectivity enable services to reach individuals and enterprises anywhere
		Cloud technology	Computing capacity, storage, and applications delivered as a service over a network or the Internet, often at substantially lower cost
		Automation of knowledge work	Intelligent software for unstructured analysis, capable of language interpretation and judgment-based tasks, potential to improve decision quality
		Digital payments	Widely accepted and reliable electronic payment systems that can bring millions of unbanked Indians out of the cash economy
		Verifiable digital identity	Digital identity that can be verified using simple methods, enabling secure delivery of payments and access to government services
Smart physical systems		Internet of Things	Networks of low-cost sensors and actuators to manage machines and objects, using continuous data collection and analysis
		Intelligent transportation and distribution	Digital services, used in conjunction with the Internet of Things, to increase efficiency and safety of transportation and distribution systems
		Advanced geographic information systems (GIS)	Systems that combine location data with other types of data to manage resources and physical activities across geographic spaces
		Next-generation genomics	Fast, low-cost gene sequencing and advanced genetic technologies to improve agricultural productivity, nutrition, and health care
Rethinking energy		Advanced oil and gas exploration and recovery	Techniques that make extraction of unconventional oil and gas (usually from shale) economical, potentially improving India's energy security
		Renewable energy	Generation of electricity from renewable sources to reduce harmful climate impact and bring power to remote areas not connected to the grid
		Advanced energy storage	Devices or systems for energy storage and management that reduce power outages, variability in supply, and distribution losses

SOURCE: McKinsey Global Institute analysis   McKinsey & Company | 0

Refer footnote 116

---

[115] Paresh Dave "Indian immigrants are tech's new titans" http://www.latimes.com/business/la-fi-indians-in-tech-20150812-story.html accessed on 25 March 2016.

[116] https://www.linkedin.com/pulse/mr-modi-goes-silicon-valley-james-manyika accessed on 25 March 2016.

Interview with Romesh Wadhwani, Founder Chairman, Symphony Technology Group, San Jose, California

The facts are compelling. Indian-Americans are now CEO's of some of the world's largest and best known global technology companies including Microsoft, Adobe, Cognizant, Harman and Bose; and Directors & Senior Executives at Google, Cisco, HP and other leading Companies. It's not too farfetched to say that most technology companies would feel great pain or even shut down if their Indians went home! The big question is, what drives the rise and success of Indian-Americans in technology? Some have said that it's Indians perseverance and work ethic; this cannot be the full answer since Chinese-American and other immigrant entrepreneurs share these qualities too. Others say it's our humility; Mr. Wadhwani said I have found that Indians are generally no more humble than their non-Indian peers! L would like to offer a different hypothesis.

According to Mr. Wadhwani we are the 1%, at least in technology. For those of us who came from India the rigorous process by which we were admitted to the IITs and other top engineering colleges in India was an effective Darwinian pre-selection process that enabled us to get graduate student visas to the US, earn degrees at the best engineering and business schools here, and then start our technology companies or join other companies with a clear advantage. Lamm convinced that even if all the faculty at the IITs retired, the students would still do well simply because they are the best and brightest India has to offer; they are intellectually curious and will learn what they need to on their own. The next generation born in the US benefits from the values of their parents, learns the importance of a great education, especially in engineering and business, and repeats this cycle.

India's IT services companies are a great incubator. Even though our IT services companies in India are doing very well, they develop woefully little proprietary intellectual property which is normally the sign of a truly great company. However, they do a great job of skilling hundreds of thousands of engineers in the basics of software and give them valuable work experience in using and integrating some of the world's best software technology and applications. When these software engineers come to the US, they have a significant advantage because they are well prepared to develop new ideas, intellectual property and software products for their US technology companies that are, in fact, IT-centric. India's loss is Google's gain!

Product is king and software trumps hardware. Mr. Wadhwani further added that there was a time when technology companies could be run by CEOs with marketing, sales, manufacturing or financial backgrounds. That era is over. Today, product is everything and software rules. Twenty years ago, the focus of technology was manufacturing-centric, dominated by Chinese-Americans. Today it's about social, mobile, analytics, cloud—all software enabled.

Google and Facebook were built into great companies by CEOs with a passion for software and web products; everything else was secondary. The strength of Indian-Americans in software engineering, their ability to communicate clearly in English, and their ability to address design and business problems with structured thinking, is a huge advantage.

The world of technology is now a world of continuous disruption. Competitors lurk in every corner, funded by aggressive venture capitalists. Markets are chaotic, break-through technologies are a constant threat. Opportunities for monetizing products can be ephemeral.

No one deals with chaos better than Indians: we are born, and grow up, in its midst; we drive in cities where drivers don't understand the concept of traffic lanes or any driving rules; we survive our complex political democracy; we deal with our social system and manage inter-personal issues with patience; we find ways to compromise; and thrive in the midst of this chaos. There's no better social preparation for success in technology.

With all these drivers of Indian-American progress and success, and with the growing population of Indian-American technology entrepreneurs, executives and engineers, we should not be surprised that the best of the best rise to become CEOs of the greatest technology companies in the world. We should be proud of India in creating and nurturing such extraordinary talent. We should be proud of the US in making such extraordinary opportunities possible to immigrants. Most of all, we should be proud of the Indian-Americans who have worked so hard and achieved so much.

Interview with Times News Service: Sujit John

In a write up provided by Sujit John he says that... the number of Indians in the top management of leading global technology companies and contributing to some great technology advances may surprise many. Consider these: four out of Google's 13-member management team are Indians—Nikesh Arora, Sundar Pichai–the man behind

Chrome and Android; Sridhar Ramaswamy and Vic Gundotra, the person behind Google+—all reporting directly to CEO Larry Page.

INTEL has Anvind Sodhani among the top seven in its executive leadership. But over the decades it also has had Indian brains behind some of its biggest technology products—Vinod Dham and Avtar Saini were key to the Pentium chip, Ajay Bhat invented the USB.

Cisco's Padmasree Warrior lays down the company's technology roadmap as CTO. VMware, the company that pioneered the technology called Virtualization that made cloud-computing possible, has four Indians in its 18-member executive leadership—Raghu Raghuram, Shekar Ayyar, Sanjay Poonen and Sanjay Mirchandani. EMC, the $22-billion data storage, analytics and cloud computing company, has three Indians among its 16 business executives; some are distinguished engineers and fellows, the highest ranks in the tech ladder.

"There weren't so many Indians at the top even in 2007 when I joined EMC," says Sarv Saravanan, senior Vice President and MD of EMC India's R&D Centre.

A couple of things have happened. One, the large number of Indians who moved to the US for higher education in the past two decades have risen up the ranks, and in some cases very rapidly because they came with the excellent background of institutions like the IITs.

Two, almost every major technology company established an R&D Centre in India in the past decade, attracted by the sea of engineering talent. Many of these have grown to become the second-largest R&D operations for those companies, accounting for at least 20% of their engineering strengths; many within these operations have become highly qualified, and there's now a near seamless movement of these technology executives between India and the US headquarters.

"India has become a breeding ground for global talent. Just over the past two weeks we were discussing how to create more global leaders out of here," says Saravanan, indicating the India phenomenon in global technology companies was only going to get bigger. Saravanan now has the additional responsibility of China, and also interacts with sales teams across Asia-Pacific to create new opportunities.

Cisco R&D demonstrates this best. Some of its senior-most talent, including Wim Elfrink, Faiyaz Shahpurwala and Anil Menon, moved to India to establish a powerful base here. When Elfrink came in 2007, there was one vice-president. Today, there are some 20-plus Vice Presidents and Senior VPs positions.

Niranjan Maka, MD of VMware India R&D, says Indians' comfort with software make them adapt very fast to changes in technology, which has kept them in good stead at a time when the world has moved rapidly to mobile devices and cloud computing. "We are also exposed to living in a hybrid culture and hence adapt very easily to an adopted environment. We can communicate extremely well, and in English—the lingua franca of modern business," he says.

Discussion with US Correspondent—Chidanand Rajghatta—The Times of India's US-based Foreign Editor, Interview in Washington

Satya Nadella's elevation as CEO of Microsoft marks the acme of global corporate leadership attained in recent years by first generation Indian immigrants. While Indra Nooyi at PepsiCo, Vikram Pandit at CitiBank (who has since stepped down), Ajay Banga at Mastercard, and Anshu Jain at Deutsche Bank have already scaled the dizzy heights, Nadella's ascension was a landmark event given Microsoft's high profile and its close association with India, fueled in part by a large section of its workforce being of Indian origin. (The figure of 33 per cent Microsofties being of Indian origin is hyperbolic; it is less than 10 per cent, and from what Bill Gates told Mr. Rajghatta several years back, it is about 20 percent in the engineering division.)

Mr. Rajghatta further added, the story of India's/Indian/ Indian-American contribution to technology is not new; it goes back at least couple of decades, possibly more. Back in the 1990s, when I was working on a book that was eventually titled "The Horse that Flew: How India's Silicon Gurus Spread Their Wings", a librarian who was helping me with research would pull my leg about India having invented zero ("THE zero," I'd correct her), as we scoured the archives for stories about Indians in the science and technology fields. The idea for the book was triggered by then "hotmail" Sabeer Bhatia's sale of Hotmail to Microsoft for $400 million. Shortly before that, Vinod Dham had been instrumental in launching the Pentium chip, and Ram Shriram (who would later fund Google and become a billionaire) was a key figure in Netscape, the early browser favorite. Years before, Narendra Singh Kapany had done pioneering work in fiber optics, C. Kumar Patel was recognized for cutting edge work on lasers, Arun Netravali led the team that developed high-definition television (HDTV), and Praveen Chaudhari held patents for the erasable read-write compact discs, the kind you burned music on a generation back.

However, Indians in the management and corporate side of things was a different deal altogether. There was the inevitable talk of a glass ceiling, and it was rare that an Indian went on to become CEO of a company, although several, like Vinod Khosla, Umang Gupta, and Kanwal Rekhi, had founded companies and even helmed them briefly. White-dominated America was leery of showing a minority face at the helm. It was only in the nifty noughties (2000 onwards) that things began to change, in keeping with the changing demographics and ethos of the US itself, and the self-belief and critical mass Indians attained, riding on the exploits of the pioneers.

In 2004, Surya Mohapatra, an alumnus of Sambalpur University and Regional Engineering College-Rourkela, his Odiya accent untainted by decades in the US, was appointed CEO of Quest Diagnostics, a Fortune 500 company. Mrs. Indra Krishnamurthy Nooyi, who went to one of her first interviews in the US in a sari after her professor advised her to "be yourself," was elevated as CEO at PepsiCo in 2006. Nagpur-born Vikram Pandit at CEO Citibank, Francisco D'Souza, son of an Indian diplomat, at Cognizant, and Adobe System's Shantanu Narayen, like Nadella a Hyderabad native, all scaled the top in 2007. Ravi Saligram at OfficeMax and Sanjay Mehrotra at SanDisk would make the grade by the end of the decade, when there were at least ten CEOs of Indian origin in the Fortune 500. The numbers compared favorably with Blacks (six CEOs), Hispanics (eight), and other Asian-Americans including Chinese, all of whose population was several times larger than that of Asian-Indians in the US.

There were several reasons attributed for this success by a number of experts to whom Mr. Rajghatta had spoken. They ranged from the Indian comfort with English and ease with numbers, to the fact that most Indian immigrants came from the relatively creamy layer of Indian society (although several achievers spoke to Mr. Rajghatta about the tough grind they went through in India, from studying by candle light to walking miles to school). It all boiled down to hard work, initiative, and a hunger for success, topped off with some luck, in an American ecosystem that recognized merit better than in India.

Mr. Rajghatta is of the opinion that fundamentally, it also went back to a society that manages the paradox of at once being religious and superstitious and at the same time fostering a scientific temper and a spirit of inquiry; or at a higher level, balancing science and spirituality. For instance, India is very familiar with Swami Vivekananda and his epic tour of America to address the Congress of Religions in Chicago in 1893. Less well known is Vivekananda's extensive engagement, pursuant to his interest in science and spirituality, with Nikola Tesla and Thomas Edison, the pioneers of all things electric.

A decade or so later, a young man named Gobind Behari Lal, a nephew of the Indian nationalist Lala Hardayal, left India to come to the University of California-Berkeley, on a scholarship. Following his post-doc, he joined Hearst Newspapers as a "science writer", the first time the designation was used in an American newspaper. In a career that lasted more than half a century, he interviewed such formidable scientific titans as Albert Einstein, Enrico Fermi and Max Planck, winning a Pulitzer Prize (1937) on the way, the first for an Indian-American (Jhumpa Lahiri would come decades later, much after Lal died in 1982). His work inspired a generation of Indian-Americans who streamed into the sciences and technology.

Little of this was known in India, which on account of its own constricting policies and a lack of opportunity, gave up some of its best and brightest to the US, which on its part used its immigration policy to attract them. From 1965 onwards, when immigration rules were relaxed for Indians, more than a million educated Indians have streamed into the US for "higher studies", many of them staying behind to become "Indian-Americans", and often, particularly in case of their children, just "Americans". Few who have been in the US for more than 20-25 years and who have taken US citizenship bear any allegiance to India, and many of them find the media hysteria in India over their achievements quite cringe-worthy.

Narayanan Krishnaswami, Sujit John and Shilpa Phadnis of TNN

In 2003, the US Department of Immigration and Naturalization Services began administering an intelligence test as part of its new immigrant survey (NIS). The test was called 'digital span', and it involved the examiners reading out lengthening sequences of numbers. Test takers were required to repeat the numbers in reverse. The test was administered to immigrant children of all nationalities, and the results were normalized into IQ scores. White Americans scored an average of 100; Ashkenazi Jews, known for their intelligence, scored an average of 110; Indian Americans scored 112.

Consider the numbers: 71% of Indian-Americans had at least a bachelor's degree as of 2010, against a US national average of 28%. As per the 2010 US census, two-thirds of Indians in the US were in professional or managerial jobs; the US average is 36%. The path to US citizenship for Indians is very different from the days of AK Mozumdar, who in 1913 had to convince a judge that he was of Caucasian origin. Indian-Americans are considered America's model minority, given their demographic and the fact that they have the lowest crime rates among all communities. But that is hardly surprising when one looks at the kind of people who immigrate to the US.

In October 2013, the private equity research firm Pitch book released a list of Universities, ranked on the basis of the number of alumni who had received a first round of VC funding. Unsurprisingly, Stanford University was at the top, followed by the University of California, Berkeley, UPenn, Harvard and others. Rounding the list, ahead of big names like Yale and Columbia, in 10th place were the IITs. Flipkart's co-founder Sachin Bansal is not surprised. "Indians, especially IITians, have always been deeply involved in the startup ecosystem in Silicon Valley, both as founders and early employees. IITs attract the top minds in the country—pushing them to excel among their highly-talented peers," he says. "IIT is a global brand now, and when you have an IIT tag, a lot of doors open for you. You get an opportunity to be in front of people who matter", says Naveen Tewari, InMobi's founder and an alumnus of IIT-Kanpur.

In the 70s and 80s, institutions like the IITs and BITS Pilani sent wave after wave of highly intelligent, well-educated students into American universities. Names like Vinod

Dham, Kanwal Rekhi and Vinod Khosla became Silicon Valley lore. They were instrumental in changing the Indian stereotype from the convenience store-keepers and motel owners to tech-savvy nerds. The premier engineering colleges were followed by others, each carving out its own niche on the backs of illustrious alumni—Manipal University's glee at Satya Nadella's ascension to the Microsoft throne being the latest example.

During the interview with Mr. Rajghatta, he added that before they became engineers and doctors, Indian students went to the US to become teachers and researchers. Prof. Shiraz Naval Minwalla is an alumnus of IIT-Kanpur and Princeton University; he taught physics at Harvard University and is now professor at the department of theoretical physics in the Tata Institute of Fundamental Research. "Things like the faculty, the quality of interactions between faculty and students, and among students, make all the difference in a university. On that count, India has no university that can compare with the likes of Harvard and Princeton. So Indians who study in good US universities become exceptional performers," he says. Prof Shrinivas Kulkarni went to the US in 1978, and has been teaching astronomy and planetary science at the California Institute of Technology since 1985. "There is still virtue in academic success in India. In the US, schools offer theatre, sports, arts, social work, and they value all of that; it's not just academics," he says. "This is a system that values education, scientific curiosity and, above all, a deep respect for learning for its own sake. The unique thing about an academic career is that it is a lifelong pursuit of all three," says Ramesh Balasubramaniam, a professor of Cognitive and Information and Science at the

University of California-Merced, explaining the lure of the American university.

While concluding Mr. Rajghatta reported that In 1999, University of California-Berkeley professor Anna Lee Saxenian found Indian-Americans were responsible for 7% of Silicon Valley startups between 1980 and 1998. By 2007, the number had gone up to 13.4% of Valley startups, and 6.5% of US startups. In 2012, as a result of recession and other factors, the overall volume of entrepreneurship dropped in the US. But Indians were still going strong: 8% of all US startups were founded by Indian-Americans. Their share of Silicon Valley startups also rose from 13.4% to 14%. "Indians are achieving extraordinary success in Silicon Valley," writes Neesha Bapat, a researcher on Silicon Valley at Stanford.

To Conclude

Indian diaspora in US has played an important role in changing US attitude. The brain drain steadily increased the number of influential Indians in the US. Indo-US economic relations and the size and clout of the Diaspora grew fast together, most prominently in Silicon Valley.

The trend now encompasses all walks of US life, including the media. It is not quite true that the brain drain is becoming the gradual takeover of the US by Indians. But it has helped transform US attitudes.[117]

---

[117] Swami Nathan S. Anklesaria Aiyar, "The hidden benefits of the brain drain" Nov. 29, 2009.
http://swaminomics.org/the-hidden-benefits-of-the-brain-drain/ accessed on 25 March 2016.

CHAPTER 7

US and India Together

In the last few years, India and US have built up the strong partnership in Commerce. With the continuation of liberal policies, India has a very high and sustained potential for fast economic growth. As India grows, further globalizes and expands, India's requirement for equipment as well as services in the areas of energy, infrastructure, technology, transportation, healthcare will increase. This situation presents diverse opportunities for US business to establish their foothold into Indian markets. Economic growth will further lead to increasing exports, creating more jobs and opportunities in India and a better life for the people. The last decade's growth in economic and commercial ties between India and US have led the strong foundation for global partnership between India and US. In this globalized world, the two largest democracies of the world have a shared fortune. Their growth and prosperity is inextricably linked. The increased trade between US and India has led to increase in the US exports to India, which supports US job market. Similarly, growing Indian investment in US is also supporting jobs across America, thus largely benefitting US workforce in every sector—high-tech industry, manufacturing and engineering jobs. For furthering this global partnership, what is required is greater trade, investment and economic partnership.

The United States and India share a strong and growing economic relationship, driven by entrepreneurial and visionary individuals, institutions, and businesses in both countries. This engagement, including trade, education, cultural, and familial ties, has always been at the leading edge of the US-India relationship and strategic partnership, and continues to expand. Our bilateral trade expanded from $19 billion in 2000 to $95 billion in 2013. US goods exports to India totaled $35 billion last year, supporting an estimated 168,000 US jobs. Cumulative Indian investment in the United States totaled $9 billion in 2012, supporting 100,000 jobs; US investment into India exceeded $28 billion, and a survey of the largest US employers in India indicates that US investment supports half a million jobs in India. Ongoing government actions to facilitate investment in both directions and open new sectors to private investment will continue to accelerate the economic growth, development, and increased prosperity that our deep economic engagement has delivered to both societies.

US and India—Trade and Economic Cooperation Fact Sheet [118]

- **The US-India Infrastructure Platform:** The US-India Infrastructure Platform is a collaborative effort between the United States and India, anchored by the two Governments and operated in concert with our private sectors, to promote US private sector engagement in India's infrastructure growth and modernization. This effort will develop concrete business opportunities through the deployment of cutting edge US technologies to meet

---

[118] http://www.state.gov/r/pa/prs/ps/2014/07/230048.htm July 31, 2014 accessed on 2 April, 2016.

India's infrastructure needs, including power, urbanization, shipping, freight transportation and other areas.

- **US-India CEO Forum:** The US-India CEO Forum is a unique gathering of CEOs and senior government officials that last met on July 12, 2013. The CEO Forum enables a forthright conversation, both about immediate policy issues to encourage greater trade and investment, as well as the longer term path for economic and business ties for our two countries. The Forum also provides an avenue for both sides to identify ways that public-private collaboration could fill gaps in the market that neither would, nor could, pursue alone. The CEO Forum has facilitated new collaborative initiatives in key areas such as cold chain, infrastructure financing, aviation, clean drinking water, and renewable energy.

- **Indo-Pacific Economic Corridor (IPEC) Strategy:** Complementing India's Enhanced Look East Policy, the United States envisions an Indo-Pacific Economic Corridor that can help bridge South and Southeast Asia—where the Indian and Pacific Oceans converge and where trade has thrived for centuries. Fostering these types of connections—physical infrastructure, regulatory trade architecture, and human and digital connectivity—will create linkages all the way from Central Asia to Southeast Asia, via South Asia. A more integrated South Asia where markets, economies, and people connect is more likely to thrive and prosper. The United States is firmly committed to the security and prosperity of the Asian continent, and connectivity, energy security, and open markets can help to realize that objective. In May 2014, the Indian Ministry of External Affairs-sponsored Research Information System for Developing Countries

Institute hosted an international conference on cross-border connectivity featuring government officials, multilateral bank representatives, and private sector firms, highlighting existing and future efforts to connect India with Southeast Asia. The United States was pleased to participate and will continue to engage in these efforts.

- **Aviation Security Equipment Testing and Evaluation Program:** Supporting the two countries' interest in increasing collaboration in the critical aviation security arena, the United States Trade and Development Agency (USTDA) is funding the first aviation security cooperation project under the US-India Aviation Cooperation Program (ACP). The technical assistance effort, also supported by the US Transportation Security Administration (TSA) and three member companies of the ACP, is designed to assist the Airports Authority of India (AAI) and India's Bureau of Civil Aviation Security (BCAS) to establish an Aviation Security Equipment Testing and Evaluation Program (ASETEP) to modernize India's aviation security environment in alignment with international standards and practices. The program will help India's civil aviation security authorities to develop clear standards for state-of-the-art aviation security equipment as well as build the technical capacity to test and certify needed systems that scan carry-on luggage, checked baggage and passengers. Under the program a delegation of Indian security officials will visit TSA testing labs focused on aviation security.

- **Regional Women's Entrepreneurship:** The United States and India continue to partner to improve economic opportunities for women. The Partnership on Women's

Entrepreneurship in Clean Energy (wPOWER), a State Department and USAID initiative, is training a network of over 1,000 women clean energy entrepreneurs to provide clean energy solutions to over 200,000 rural households. Launched in December 2012, the South Asia Women's Entrepreneurship Symposium (SAWES) initiative is promoting cross-border partnerships to improve access to finance, markets, and capacity-building for women entrepreneurs across South and Central Asia. USAID also supports the Indian Self-Employed Women's Association (SEWA) to provide vocational skills and leadership training to Afghan women. USAID is now expanding this initiative.

• **Tourism, Travel and Visas:** In 2013, over 850,000 Indians visited the United States, and over one million Americans visited India, the largest group of foreign arrivals. The US Mission in India has expanded its consular staffing and invested over $100 million in updating and expanding consular facilities to facilitate travel to the United States, processing ninety-seven percent of visa applications in one business day.

• **Higher Education:** Higher education is a vital part of our economic engagement. Indian students comprise the second-largest group of foreign students in the United States, with approximately 100,000 students studying in the United States in 2012-13. These students contribute over $3 billion to the US economy every year, creating one American job for every three students. They advance innovation and research in our universities. With support from the US-India Higher Education Dialogue, US community colleges partner with Indian institutions to enhance economic opportunity in India through adoption of the community college education model and skills development best practices. The Higher Education Dialogue also creates enhanced opportunities for student and scholar mobility and faculty collaboration between the United States and India, as well as exchanges on technology-enabled learning. USAID supports the India-Support for Teacher Education Project which provides a three-month, customized training for 110 Indian teacher educators at Arizona State University's Mary Lou Fulton Teachers College, enabling the teacher educators to offer high quality training to Indian teachers upon their return.

• **Education Research Partnerships:** The 21st Century Knowledge Initiative supports partnerships between higher education institutions in both countries to strengthen teaching and research in priority fields such as energy, climate change, and public health. The United States and India have each pledged $5 million to this Initiative. The Fulbright-Nehru program has nearly tripled since 2009, with approximately 300 Indian and US students and scholars participating annually, making it the largest Fulbright Scholar Program in the world. Since 1950, the United States-India Education Foundation (USIEF) has awarded approximately 9,600 Fulbright grants funded by the US Department of State in a full range of academic disciplines. USIEF has also administered 8,600 other awards, including the US Department of Education's Fulbright-Hays and the East-West Center grants, for a total of over 18,000 awards in the last 64 years.

- **Strengthening Best Practices in Manufacturing:** Identifying mechanisms for sharing best practices is essential to promoting commercial cooperation between India and the United States. By sharing best practices in innovation and economic development strategies with India's Ministry of Urban Development through the National Institute of Standards and Technology's Manufacturing Extension Partnership (NIST-MEP) and the Economic Development Administration (EDA), the US Department of Commerce seeks to strengthen partnerships with the Government of India and the Indian business community, focusing on infrastructure development, manufacturing and supply chain integration, skills development and business climate. NIST-MEP and EDA will host visits by Indian senior level officials to its MEP centers and EDA investment sites as part of this effort.

- **Investment Promotion:** SelectUSA and the Export-Import Bank of India cemented a partnership on July 30th. Both organizations will work together to assist Indian companies and entrepreneurs as they seek to invest and create jobs in the United States. The US Department of Commerce also expressed appreciation to the Indian investors who participated in the SelectUSA 2013 Investment Summit, and committed to working with Indian officials and industry associations to recruit a strong delegation from India for the March 2015 Investment Summit.

- **The US-India Commercial Dialogue:** The Commercial Dialogue provides a forum in which both governments and the Indian and US private sectors can collaborate on issues of mutual interest, thereby ensuring that our trade relationship continues to grow and diversify. The US Department of Commerce and India's Ministry of Commerce and Industry have taken steps to renew the Commercial Dialogue for an additional two-year term until March 2016. Both sides share a strong interest in broadening the Dialogue engagement and are exploring new areas of cooperation, including encouraging the private sector to work with the governments on round-tables to promote innovation in advanced manufacturing.

- **Trade Policy Forum:** The Trade Policy Forum (TPF) enables the United States and India to engage on a wide range of policy issues impacting bilateral trade and investment. As part of an ongoing commitment to strengthen this dialogue, both governments hope to renew expert-level discussions on trade and investment policy issues of interest to the two countries such as intellectual property and investment in manufacturing. The TPF's Private Sector Advisory Group (PSAG), composed of US and Indian private sector leaders, plans to provide input to both governments.

In her remarks in New York City, US Assistant Secretary Nisha Desai Biswal said, with the ongoing strong partnership in commerce, over the past few years, India has become the second fastest growing source of foreign direct investment into the United States. In addition, two-way trade has nearly tripled from $36 billion in 2005 to $104 billion in 2014, as the two countries work towards a planned $500 billion in trade. Today, there are more than 500 US companies active in India, leading to an increase in employment. Also, the number of Indian companies operating in the United States has increased from roughly 85 companies in 2005 to more than 200 companies today.[119]

Though trade between India and US is greater than before, US trade with China is exceedingly more, which proves that there is still a great potential for trade growth between India and US. Complete implementation of Civil Nuclear Agreement, cooperation in defence trade and technology and moving forward towards Bilateral Investment Treaty will facilitate more US investment in India and more Indian investments in US. President Obama, in his address on 26th January 2015 had focussed on some specific areas in order to realise the full potential of US-India economic partnership.

1. For the ease of Indian Business to establish in US "Select US" initiative to cut red tape and streamline regulation

2. Reforms to overcome the barriers including bureaucratic restrictions within India , one of which is the establishment of new governmental committee dedicating to fast tracking American investment and creating transparent, consistent and predictable business environment.

3. US assistance to India to develop new technologies for clean energy, upgrading transport structure, improving internet connectivity within India and between India and the outside world, digitalization of bank accounts, public-private partnership initiatives to facilitate Indian-Americans to directly invest in India and financing Indian business as well as in the rural development.

4. The objective of inclusive and sustained growth that requires expanding solar energy and access to electricity

---

[119] Mina Fabulous "Us and India Doing Well Together in Business", August 14, 2015, http://newsblaze.com/world/south-asia/us-and-india-doing-well-together-in-business_39639/ accessed on 25 March 2016.

in rural areas, access to clean water, improving the quality of air by controlling pollution, thus leading to environmentally sound development.

India's economic advancement has brought India to the status of a truly global power. India's role in shaping the international system is expanded. In Asia-Pacific as well as in Afghanistan, India and US have shared interest in the peaceful, growing and prosperous region. India and US have entered into a strategic partnership—deeper defence and security ties and the partnership can become the closest in the region.

CHAPTER 8

100 Days of Trump's Presidency– Looking Forward

Source: US Consulate General

After almost a year and half long battle, Donald Trump became the 45th President of the United States of America. His campaign team should thank in part the surprise victories from several States that stunned all the Election Pundits and prognosticators who had very little hope of Donald J. Trump emerging victorious. This election had sent shock waves across 50 States and ripples beyond America's shores.

A leading Commentator on US Elections stated that despite President Barack Obama's successful efforts to cut unemployment rates and spur economic growth after the great recession of 2008, the white blue-collar men and women of America, especially in the mid-west, felt a sense of isolation from the distant machinations of Washington and were frustrated by lack of opportunities for upward economic and social mobility. In Mr. Trump, they found a leader who not only promised to make America great again. Once this bond was forged between the white masses and their messiahs, the rest was history.[120]

The country saw a Presidential candidate who called his campaign a "Movement" and its slogan was "Make American Great Again" offering the angry multitudes hope for the future.[121] There was no ideology here, no out flowing of new and revolutionary ideas, but only simplistic, repetitive incantations about his competitor Hillary was corrupt and ineffectual, that the legacy of Obama administration, especially Obama Care, needed reversal and that Muslims entry into the US should be rigorously monitored and even prevented. The world witnessed the biggest political upset in US Election history.

After being declared a victor, Mr. Trump's acceptance speech was subdued, inclusive and humble. He promised to bind the wounds of the nation and also promising respect for and friendship with other communities around the world.

---

[120] http://www.thehindu.com/opinion/op-ed/Imagining-Trump%E2%80%99s-America/article16441023.ece, December 02, 2016 visited January 5 2017.
[121] Nirupama Rao, "November thunderbolt" http://www.thehindu.com/opinion/lead/November-thunderbolt/article16274182.ece, November 10, 2016 visited on January 7, 2017.

April 29, 2017—100 Days of Trump's Presidentship

On 29th April President Trump completed his 100 days in office. The brief review of this period suggests that the road ahead for Trump is full of obstacles. This is because it is becoming increasingly difficult for him to keep the promises he made before elections. Different examples can be sighted such as the Healthcare Bill (Which is passed with some modifications and amendments in Congress recently), the court blocked on his decision to restrict the entry of travellers from Muslim countries, some evidences of Russian active collaboration during elections and the resultant action taken against his National Security Advisor, continued pop ups of several other problems in his administration and the resultant lower approval ratings for President Trump, his lack of respect for the institutions and so on. 100 days of his Presidency also made him learn a very important lesson—Business and Politics are not one and the same. The Constitution, the Parliament, the Judiciary and also the members of his own party are the controllers and President cannot enjoy absolute control making politics unlike business. This has casted doubts about whether he will be successful in keeping his promises and "can get the things done" in true sense of the term. In the near future President Trump will be tested on how he is able to handle global powers, global competitors and global adversaries.

Pre-Election Foreign Policy Proclamations of President Trump

The foreign policy "statements" of Trump appeared to be very aggressive from the beginning. He demanded that US Allies in Europe and Asia share more of the burden for common security. He expressed his willingness to accept Japan and

South Korea going nuclear in defending themselves against China and North Korea respectively. Mr. Trump was open to cutting a deal with Russia in stepping up the fight against the ISIS in the Middle East.

Trump promised to scrap the nuclear deal with Iran negotiated by President Obama. He promised to redress economic hardships at home, offered to strengthen the US borders. Trump shook the long standing domestic political coalitions of US and laid out a different direction for America. He declared that North Korea would need careful and urgent focus as also relationships with China and also Russia especially in the context of Syrian issue.

100 DAYS IN OFFICE

PROMISES KEPT

Donald Trump made a string of promises during his campaign to be the 45th president of the US. Here's a fact-check on some of the promises kept and broken as he marks 100 days in office on Saturday

- Pull out of Trans-Pacific Partnership
- Ban White House officials from lobbying for foreign govts
- Appoint a conservative judge to supreme court

WORK IN PROGRESS
- Appoint a conservative judge to supreme coDeporting all illegal imigrants
- Reform tax system, bring back jobs
- Cancel funds to UN climate programmes, withdraw from Paris deal
- Renegotiate trade deals like Nafta
- Bomb 'the hell out of IS' terror group
- Lift curbs on production of oil, shale energy & coal
- Increase the size of military

PROMISES NOT KEPT
- Repeal and replace Obamacare
- A border wall paid for by Mexico
- Ban on all Muslims entering US
- Label China a currency manipulator
- Prosecure Hillary Clinton over use of pvt email server
- Abandoning 'obsolete' alliance Nato
- Freeze on all federal hiring
- Hands-off approach on Syria
- Approve waterboarding,
- Massive rebuilding of US infrastructure
- Shift US embassy in Israel to Jerusalem from Tel Aviv

Source: American Library, New Delhi

Relations between India and US—Speculations before the Presidential Elections

Before the results of Presidential elections were out, there was a lot of discussion about US relations with India under a "New President". The political analysts were of the opinion that if Mrs. Clinton would come to power, the relations between India and US would improve further. Their conclusion was based on the fact that Mrs. Clinton always had played a significant role in improving the relationship between India and US. She was the backbone of India-US Civil Nuclear Deal during the President ship of Mr. Clinton and had also played an important role in improving ties between India and US during the two terms of Obama Administration. Hence if Mrs. Clinton would have emerged as the new face, it would have been new face of India-US relations, not merely as "allies" but as "partners" who are equals.

Though, Republican Party of United States had always been in favour of friendly relations with India, the Presidential candidate of Republic Party, Mr. Trump seemed to be problematic. President Donald Trump, during his campaign pitched for several things, including a rewrite of the US Immigration Policy. The political analysts had predicted that the US foreign and domestic policy would change dramatically if Mr. Trump comes to power. This prediction was the result of the extreme views of Mr. Trump regarding Pakistan, China, granting H1B Visa, refuges and migrators, Muslims and terrorism. Initially this was seen as partly pro Indian, but, his mimicry of Indian employees in the call centres made them conclude that Mr. Trump, though, did not seem to be anti-Indian, he is also not very pro-Indian. So it was predicted by the political analysts that if Mr. Trump comes to power it will be very difficult to predict the direction in which India-US relations will move.

The Future of India-US Relations

During Hillary Clinton's tenure as Secretary of State (2011), she had announced the rebalancing to Asia which was not elucidated or effectively deployed by the Obama administration. Mr. Trump is of the view that free trade deals have destroyed working class America. As a result, the Trans Pacific Partnership Trade Agreements will be an aborted deal. For the new President one major challenge will be how to pursue a stable and intelligent relationship with a highly militarized China that sees diminished US Economic Power and military capability as an opportunity to advance its territorial claims in maritime Asia.

Mrs. Nirupama Rao, former Indian Ambassador to US stated that Mr. Trump is a proclaimed opponent of terrorism and his approach to Pakistan and its support of various terror groups will be no nonsense and adversarial. Ms. Rao further stated that his policy and attitude to India is expected to be positive and welcoming maintaining the decade long positive ties. His connections with the Indian American community and his general view that "India is doing Great" suggest that he is well inclined to further cement the India-US Partnership.

During the first 100 days of President Trump there have taken place high level diplomatic visits and meetings between India and US. There are several important concerns such as H1B visa that will directly affect the Indian Tech industry and the tax cut proposals which will have an indirect impact on India because of the increase in US trade deficits and resultant increase in the interest rates. However Just 100 days are insufficient to arrive at the long term conclusions about India-US relations.

In an interview with Mr. Kumar, Founder Chairman, The Republican Hindu Coalition (RHC) and a Chicago based industrialist, he expressed his opinions about the future of India-US relationship

According to him, President Trump is essentially a businessman, and one of his principal goals will be expand trade with India from the current $100 billion to $300 billion. Under the new administration the US economy is expected to grow by 4-5 per cent and there will be all kinds of work both for US and non US citizens. The US does need a lot of IT workers from India. Due to H1B visa issue and the suggested reforms, minimum wages will go up for foreign workers and Indian Companies may have to shell out higher wages. President Trump wants to bring back jobs lost to outsourcing. This will have direct bearing on the Indian IT Industry. The Indian IT Industry makes about 60 per cent of its $100 Billion revenue from US through jobs outsourced by Companies in America. Thus, the waters may be turbulent for some time but the problems will be resolved gradually. However, given the large contribution of the Indian IT Industry to the US Economy through taxes and CSR contributions, Trump may not come down heavily.

New Challenges

The Indian IT Industry has in fact down played the impact of the rules. Industry experts feel that though the policy will increase scrutiny, the move is on expected lines.

The Indian IT Sector is already facing multiple challenges-from a shrinking pie for its traditional services business, increasing competition and narrowing margins. It is clear that Indian IT Companies will have to do a lot of local hiring. The big five Indian IT Companies may be more successful in being able to get the necessary talent as they have been spending on brand building in the US too.

IT Industry body NASSCOM is all set to revise growth for the sector to single digits in 2016-17. Now if US based Companies are forced to limit outsourcing, there may be a bigger risk for these Companies. A NASSCOM report says that the industry pays equal wages to US Nationals as well as Indians on H1B visas. In 2013, while a US Citizen was paid about $84,447 a year for his work, an H1B visa holder was paid $81,447 a year with an additional $15,000 on visa and ticket costs for the individual and his spouse/family. It adds that it is talent shortage in the US that compels the American Companies to hire talent from India. NASSCOM quotes a report that shows that 46 percent of openings in TTEN jobs go unfilled for more than a month in the US. Under these circumstances, New Delhi must look beyond accusations of protectionism against the US or claiming an entitlement for even more visas for Indians and rethink a mutually beneficial partnership that has sustained support in both the countries.

Prospective Indo-US Trade Relations Under Trump Regime

The election of Donald Trump as US President may bring some level of uncertainty in the Indo US trade relations due to the conflicting stances that he took during the campaigning.

Trump's statements on Protectionism may affect the trade relationship.

There are two things to be observed. First is Trump's focus on domestic manufacturing and increasing local employment and second his focus on bilateral trade agreements with various countries. Trump has already made statements against the Multi-lateral treaties such as the proposed Transatlantic Trade and Investment Partnership (TTIP) and North American Free Trade Agreements (NAFTA). Mr. Trump has said that he will renegotiate all bilateral deals that will be more favourable to US manufacturing. The most important is that the US would not be bound by WTO rules and rulings by WTO Courts. This can turn India's commercial ties with its largest trading partner more contentious according to an International Trade Expert and US official.

The US is India's leading trading partner. In 2015-16, almost 16% of India's total export was absorbed by the US market. India exported $41 billion worth of goods to the US and imported a little over $22 billion from there. Major products exported include textiles, precious stones, and pharmaceutical products. One knowledgeable observer of the trade scenario opined that if Multi-lateral treaties such as NAFTA which offers major export tariff concessions to other countries like Mexico are repealed by the Trump Administration, India may find an opening to increase export of its Textile products to the US.

Indian Pharmaceutical companies which have USA as their major market have been facing considerable hassles from the USFDA in the last few years. Pharma issues are primarily regulatory issues. It is interesting to note that

Trump also advocated cancelling the Obama Care under the Government health care net. It is not clear how it may affect the Indian pharmaceutical companies. But it is evident that Indian companies have specialized in exporting generic drugs to the US market. This demand may not be affected as the supply chain lines would have to be maintained.

Ms. Moushami Joshi, International Trade Lawyer with Pillsbury Winthrop Shaw Pitman, a well-known Washington Law firm, said that the US will be difficult partner to work with, particularly at the WTO. The Trump Administration's drive to reduce American trade deficit will bring India into sharp focus. "The emphasis on opening the market for US Agricultural Products and Intellectual Property are of particular significance for India" said Ms. Moushami. She further added that the push for Agriculture directly affects India.

Indian GST and US Government Viewpoint—Stepping Up Economic Engagement

In the recent public gathering of US India Importers Council in Mumbai. The US Consul General gave a perspective of the current state of US India trade relations and the impact on the private sector of the new GST regime and how it may affect US investment and exports. Indian economy is the fastest growing major economy in the world with rapidly growing middle class and increasing consumer spending. American products are in high demand as Indian consumer is becoming more discerning and demanding in view of increased purchasing power.

The US Government is a strong supporter of Make in India. Many American Companies like GE, Johnson & Johnson,

Ford, etc. have been part of India for long time and are proud to be part of "Make in India" success story.

The Consul General told the gathering that they are inundated with requests from American Companies seeking assistance for finding partners and clients for their products. The two way trade between India and US stands at US $110 billion and now a goal has been set to grow the trade relationship to over US $500 billion in the coming years. GST is viewed by America as one of the right step in this direction. GST will unify the Indian market making it more transparent and accountable thereby enabling easier business relationship with India. The myriad of taxes viz., customs, excise, sales, service, luxury, etc. to be dealt with by the suppliers, retailers and consumers and neither do they receive offset benefits for taxes already paid on inputs in their value chain. The GST will eliminate the cascading burden of tax on tax and double taxation experienced by Companies.

The US e-Commerce and Logistics companies have shown strong interest in GST as this will reduce cross border transit time and overall transportation cost. Manual tax filing will give way to process on line with planned GST infrastructure which will reduce corruption and create cost and time efficiencies.

The United States is committed to supporting India's efforts to improve the ease of doing business and streamline the regulatory environment for trade.

Indo-US Strategic and Defence Ties

When Mr. Donald Trump occupies the White House, bilateral defence and strategic ties with India are likely to undergo a strategic shift with increased military purchases and geo political moves. Defence trade between India and the US presently stands at US $15 billion from a mere $200 million in 2000.[122]

In August, India and US signed one of the three crucial foundational agreements—Logistics.

Exchange Memorandum of Agreement (LEMOA) that will enable their respective militaries to collaborate together and allow each other's defence bases for repair and replenishment.[123] The US signs these foundational agreements with countries that it considers strategically important. However, it remains to be seen whether the Trump Administration will urge India to sign the remaining two agreements viz., Communications and Information Security Memorandum of Agreements for Geo Spatial Information and Services Co-operation—as vehemently as the previous government. The US is also well aware of the fact that India is the world's largest importer of defence equipment, accounting for 15 per cent of the total global weapons imports in the last five years.

However, defence experts opined that Trump's victory is expected to bring some element of uncertainty in global geopolitical order. We do not know as to how under Trump's regime, the relationship between the US and Russia or US and Iran are going to be and that will be the key. It is well known by now that when it comes to Pakistan and issues such as cross border terrorism, Trump will be a close ally of India.

---

[122]Nayanima Basu, "India-US strategic, defence ties will undergo paradigm shift" http://www.thehindubusinessline.com/news/world/visited on 12/5/17.

[123]Varghese K. George, "India, US sign military logistics pact" www.thehindu.com/news/international/ visited on 12/5/17.

Traditionally Republican administrators have been better for India when it comes to India-Pakistan ties. But no US administration can ignore Pakistan. And India has to realize that India-Pakistan ties have to be managed by these two countries and not by the US.

Steps to Strengthen India US Economic Engagement[124]

In an interview with Mr. Rick Rossow, Senior Adviser, Wadhwani Chair in US India Policy Studies, Centre for Strategic and International Studies (CSIS), Washington DC, he explained that under Trump Administration, US Foreign Policy is about to shift in a new direction. US India ties have steadily improved over the last three years—particularly in the defense and security sector. Yet there are important ways that US and India can strengthen existing dialogues and create new channels that will amplify the impact of US India partnership on our economic engagement.

1. **Be more Responsive to India's Agenda:** President Trump has evolved a program to safeguard US jobs by giving incentives to US Companies so that manufacturing gets a boost and jobs are created in the US. He has used a combination of coercion and tough discussions with the CEOs of large Corporations to keep jobs in the US. At the same time for United States co-operation with India is bet on the future, both in terms of India's expected economic and security role. It is a major customer for US products and services especially in the hi-tech area. With this in mind, US should ensure that new programs

---

[124] US-India Insight: Eight Ways to Strengthen US-India Cooperation in 2017.
January 12, 2017, https://www.csis.org/analysis/us-india-insight-eight-ways-strengthen-us-india-cooperation-2017 visited on 12/5/17.

and ideas are conceived, based, atleast partly as a response to major Indian programs. The Modi Government has a number of high profile initiatives, such as "Make in India", "Digital India, "Smart Cities", "Clean India" and "Start Up India". These initiatives are quite broad and we can find meaningful ways to engage with each other that simultaneously meets US interests. On the other hand, presenting ideas to the Government of India that are not related to India's major initiates has sometimes created difficulties. This also applies to Indian Companies presenting their proposals to US Government. It facilitates existing initiatives and ensures smooth co-ordination, the US government should ensure that key US Government positions based in India are filled quickly. The US Embassy in New Delhi is without an Ambassador for the last 5 months.

2. **Build a Long Term Game Plan on Trade:** The United States and India are unable to taking a more proactive position on global trade matters. A range of obstacles lie in the way of a more proactive Indian stance on trade, not the least of which is India's large goods trade deficit— averaging 8 per cent of GDP over the last five years. The United States should develop a long term plan on trade engagement that will pair US co-operation with incremental steps on the way to trade integration. In some ways, the US "reset" initiated on defense trade after losing the Medium Multi Role Combat Aircraft bid in 2011 is a model; it resulted in programs like the Defense Technology and Trade Initiative (DTTI) and has helped lead the growth in US Defense business in India.

3. **Engage more with Government of India, Ministry of Finance:** Many US Commercial Policy lie within

the domain of Ministry of Finance. Yet many of the formal dialogues on trade and commerce matters have relatively little direct connectivity with the Ministry of Finance, apart from the US India Financial and Economic Partnership (co-lead by the US Department of Treasuries).

4. **Engage with Indian State Leaders:** In the last 24 months, we say an uptick in the number of US Programs that seek to engage India's powerful State leaders. This effort should be deepened and widened. Ultimately, the power to achieve India's developmental goals lie with India's powerful State leaders more than the Central Government. Building stronger relationships with regional parties that control many Indian States will also act as an important buffer if there is ever a downturn in relations between New Delhi and Washington.

5. **Expand Homeland Security Co-operation:** The United States and India have had a "Homeland Security Dialogue" since 2011 though the Governments have not been able to meet on a consistent basis at the ministerial level. India and the United States share an enormous range of concerns in this area, from aviation security to coast guard development and there is wide latitude for dialogue. Past experience shows, however, that initiatives will succeed only if they are pushed through high level engagement. A major terrorist attack on the Indian soil coordinated from Pakistan, resulting in a significant Indian military response is also one of the more likely factors to derail India's rise as an economic and security partner of the United States, thus hindering economic engagement between two great democracies. Helping

India strengthen itself against such attacks is strongly in the US interest.

6. **Discuss Tax Policy Concerns regularly:** Tax disputes make up a sizeable portion of US Commercial disputes. Apart from the formal "Mutual Agreement Procedure" negotiations, it is notable that the "Financial and Economic partnership" between Treasury Department and Ministry of Finance has started to include tax issues.

7. **Bring an impressive Delegation to the Global Entrepreneurship Summit:** India has agreed to host this important annual summit in 2017. Founded by the US Government, both USA and India should make the Summit a core highlight of our global partnership in 2017, with a powerful 100 member US Delegation composed of public and private leaders who will discuss new age business sectors whereby India and US can step up their economic engagement. This will help to achieve the dream of reaching US$ 500 Billion in two way trade in the next 5 years.

8. **Engage Opposition Leaders:** The United States should make sure it continues to engage regularly with the BJP leadership so as to maintain good momentum. It should also maintain contact with the opposition leaders so that in future if the course changes, it will be in a neutral position.

Important to the success of the ideas above, the Trump administration must also have senior level champions of the relationship. US India ties, while strengthening, still require regular high level engagement from US Officials to achieve concrete objectives. This relationship cannot thrive if placed on autopilot.

Looking Forward

While congratulating President Trump on his victory, Prime Minister Narendra Modi said "We appreciate the friendship you have articulated towards India during your campaign. We look forward to working with you closely to take India US bilateral ties to a new height."

The US and India are friendly nations and the world's largest free market democracies. The basis of this gracious relationship between India and US is no doubt the increasing economic engagement between the two.

The relationship, which started developing especially in the new millennium, rests on four pillars. The first pillar is cooperation in the areas of Trade and Business and expanding private sector investment. US companies like Pepsi have shown a greater interest in investing in India by understanding our rules and regulations and Ford Motors is in the process of completing its largest manufacturing plant in Gujarat. Even Indian companies have invested in US, thus creating jobs for thousands of Americans. Bilateral business, commerce and trade are the driving force in the economic engagement between the world's two great democracies. The second pillar is the Professional and student exchanges. One lakh plus Indian students in US and a very strong Indian Diaspora in high offices are a strength in partnership. The third pillar is greater cooperation on regional and global issues and priorities. Due to the changing geo-political conditions in West Asia and the emergence of ISIS, new challenges have come to the forefront. The challenge posed by the fundamentalist forces in the region is global in nature and the two strong democracies need to cooperate on these global issues. The other issues that need cooperation range from nuclear liability to climate change. The forth pillar is the expanding security and military cooperation. India is expected to play an important role in democratization process in post 2014 Afghanistan. There is also an agreement about the sale of defence equipment by US companies which could be co-developed and co-produced in India under a more simple regulatory process.

In all these years, the US-India relations have withstood the test of times with challenges arising at every nook and corner of this journey. There were setbacks in the relationship between India and US arising out of the arrest of the Indian Diplomat and the US Trade Representative reviewing India's intellectual property regime. It was suspected that those issues would bring a new twist in the relationship. However, fortunately, those issues were handled effectively at the diplomatic level. In fact, the ways, the issues have been handled prove that the relationship between the two largest democracies of the world is becoming more and more mature.

Today, world system is facing number of challenges, which are global in nature. Global economic downturn, terrorism, religious fundamentalism, climate change and such other issues have made it mandatory for the nation states to adopt cooperative strategies to deal with them. India and US are no exception to that.

As the economic engagement between the two has fully fledged, the economic interests of both rule all other forms of affiliations. The number of jobs in manufacturing sector in US has been taken over by China in last 15 years. In the present condition of economic slump in US, the manufacturing sector of US needs a boost and US cannot afford to ignore India that has the large consumer based economy.

Further, US and India have a common concern, China. The aggressive policies of China in South China Sea and Indian Ocean and the One Belt, One Route project have initiated Indo-US cooperation in strategic affairs and in the field of maritime security. US views India as its most significant strategic partner in South Asia. As India and US share common perceptions about several world problems ranging from climate change and global health to peacekeeping and cyber governance, both aim at creating set of norms for the rule based world order. Presidential elections will not impact these perceptions.

The one thing is clear, there is no possibility of about turn in the relationship between India and US. The relationship between India and US had been strengthened significantly over past few years. As a result, it can be predicted that even the Trump regime will not affect the relationship broadly. The impact may be only issue based. So if the relations change, the change will be for the better, or else, the relations will continue on the same path, may not immediately moving in the upward direction.

Bibliography

Books

1. Barrett, W. "Trump: The Greatest Show on Earth: The Deals, the Downfall, the Reinvention" (2016).

2. Bhatnagar, Subhash. "India's software industry." Technology, Adaptation, and Exports (2006): 49.

3. Cohen, Stephen P., and Dhruva Jaishankar. "Indo-US Ties: The Ugly, the Bad and the Good." Washington, DC: The Brookings Institution, February (2009).

4. D'Antonio, Michael. The Truth about Trump. Macmillan, 2016.

5. D'Costa, Anthony, and Eswaran Sridharan, eds. India in the global software industry: Innovation, firm strategies and development. Springer, 2003.

6. Latif, S. Amer, and Amb Karl F. Inderfurth. "US-India Defense Trade: Opportunities for deepening the partnership." US-India Insight 2.7 (2012).

7. Mohan, C. Raja. Crossing the rubicon: The shaping of India's new foreign policy. Viking Adult, 2003.

8. Mohanty, Deba R., and Uma Purushothaman. India-US Defence Relations: In Search of a Direction. Observer Research Foundation, 2011.

9. Saxena, Mili and Padmini Ravindra Nath. "Global Economic Recession and its implications for Indo-US Trade." OJAS: 47.

10. Shukla, Subhash. Foreign policy of India. Anamika Pub & Distributors, 2007. Trump, Donald J., and Tony Schwartz. Trump: The art of the deal. Ballantine Books, 2009.

Articles/Reports

1. Bukhari, Syed Shahid Hussain. "India-United States strategic partnership: Implications for Pakistan." Berkeley Journal of Social Sciences 1.1 (2011).

2. Campaign Papers—NY Times, Washington Post, India Abroad.

3. Cohen, Stephen P. "India and America: An Emerging Relationship." Conference on the Nation-State System and Transnational Forces in South Asia. Vol. 8. No. 10. 2000.

4. Collection of US Presidents Inaugural Speeches—Library of Congress.

5. Congressional Reports on US Elections.

6. CSIS Reports, Washington DC.

7. Forbes, Bloomberg; Ethics Agreements; quartz.

8. Kapur, S. Paul, and Sumit Ganguly. "The transformation of US-India relations: an explanation for the rapprochement and prospects for the future." Asian Survey 47.4 (2007): 642-656.

9. Kaye, Charles R., Joseph S. Nye Jr, and Alyssa Ayres. Working with a Rising India: A Joint Venture for the New Century. Council on Foreign Relations Press, 2015.

10. Library of Congress Reports, Washington DC.

11. McDevitt, Michael A., M. Taylor Fravel, and Lewis M. Stern. "The Long Littoral Project: South China Sea." CNA Report, viewed April 3.2013 (2013): 28.

12. Mohan, C. Raja. "Modi's American Engagement." Seminar, 2015.

13. Mohan, C. Raja. "Rising India: partner in shaping the global commons?." The Washington Quarterly 33.3 (2010): 133-148.

14. Nandy, Debasish. "Indo-US Economic Relations (1991-1999): A Realistic Engagement."

15. Nayak, Polly. US Security Policy in South Asia Since 9/11-Challenges and Implications for the Future. Asia-Pacific Center for Security Studies Honolulu Hi, 2005.

16. Nguyen, Hang Thuy Thi. "Robert G. Sutter. The United States and Asia: Regional Dynamics and Twenty First Century Relations." European journal of American studies (2016).

17. Pant, Harsh V. "China's Naval Expansion in the Indian Ocean and India-China Rivalry. The Asia-Pacific Journal, Japan Focus Volume 8.18 (2010).

18. Redden, Mark E., and Michael P. Hughes. Global Commons and Domain Interrelationships: Time for a New Conceptual Framework? (Strategic Forum, October 2010). National Defense Univ Washington DC Inst for National Strategic Studies, 2010.

19. Reports of White House Press Correspondents Association.

20. Shukla, Ajai. "India-US Defence Ties Grow with Assertive Modi Govt." Business Standard India 21 (2015).

21. Singh, Abhijit. "Malabar 2015: Strategic Power Play in the Indian Ocean." The Diplomat (2015).

22. Singh, Hemant Krishan, and Tincy Sara Solomon. "BIT and Beyond" (2013).

23. Subramanian, Arvind. "Congressional Testimony" (2011).

24. US International Trade Commission. "Trade, Investment, and Industrial Policies in India: Effects on the US Economy" (2014).

25. Vinod K. and Kamlesh Jain. "How America Benefits from Economic Engagement with India." by India-US World affairs Institute, Inc., available online at: http://www. iaccindia. com/userfiles (2010).

26. Wall Street Journal Review.

27. White House Press Statements and Reuters Reports.

www.ingramcontent.com/pod-product-compliance
Lightning Source LLC
Chambersburg PA
CBHW072237270326
41930CB00010B/2161